Your Personal Book of

Let charming rhythms of Blues flow from your fingertips, freely improvise Blues!

Scott Su

Fundamental,

Advanced & Improvisation

Translated by
Lynda Huang

[FOREWORDS]

It has been nearly 20 years since my first experience in Blues. From feeling rusty and unfamiliar with Blues in the beginning to being able to improvise Blues freely, I then have come to a point and realize that for allowing the soul of music to be truly a different type of charm, I will need to undergo a long state of soaking and self-refined.

During the time periods of my learning, in addition to non-stoppingly listening and playing Blues music, I also read many Blues method books and materials, and thus learned very much. I also have **discovered important matters which many method books have not yet explained.** Thus, I have decided to write down all my thoughts and feelings throughout the years of learning Blues music systemized with a goal which aims for being capable of fingerstyle Blues improvisation playing alone. I sincerely hope that whoever is serious about learning Blues, and guitarists who want to play Blues better, there's more room for learning to think and practice.

In order to play Blues well, you would need to be immersed in listening and practices. Therefore I have arranged and created a great volume of demonstrations and etudes on a basis of a 12-measure as one unit, and I look forward to that reader can build up a certain level of Blues playings by studying this book. Regardless of fingerstyle or simply improvisations on progressing melodies, as long as you are willing to spend time to execute practicing thoroughly, to comprehend and to think, this book is your practical help to increase performance levels in Blues music.

Welcome to the world of Blues!

Scott Su

> Please visit Scott's official website: scottsu.net for MP3 demo downloads, or listen on Youtube.

Author

Scott Su, an independent music composer, producer and guitarist. He is also a richly-experienced studio musician, skillful in music arrangements and releases mainly guitar performance albums. His self- composed albums include "Are You Still There?", a guitar performance single and "No Flowers On Island." Scott also writes useful guitar method books which include "Fretboard Secret Handbook" ,
"Playing Guitar So Easy" , "Your Training Notebook on Pop Special Chord Progressions" and etc.

Site: http://tw.ScottSu.net/
Facebook: http://www.facebook.com/scottmusic

「Are You Still There?」

A new acoustic guitar performance single

Compose / Arrangement / Performance / Recording / Mixing / Production by Scott Su, Harmonica by Otis Tsao

「No Flowers On Island」

Electric / Acoustic guitar performance album

Compose / Arrangement / Performance / Recording / Mixing / Production by Scott Su

[Table of Contents]

Chapter THREE :

Thinkings and Improvisations of Advanced Blues —— 84

Conclusions

Solo Fingerstyle

Blues Guitar

There are four elements in music: melody, harmony, rhythm and timbre. Thus, in order to find clear elements in Blues music, we will need to identify the main characteristics which can help us learn faster.

Chapter ONE

Basic Learnings of Blues

◈ Blues Music

When we would like to learn a completely different song style, it is very necessary for you to start learning from listening to music. After hearing and feeling different song styles, you then can be more capable of identifying whether your playing actually expresses the feelings of that particular song style. It is simply like learning a new language, taking the English language as one quick example, you will need to listen to people of different English-speaking countries to speak English with various accents so you know and can hear whether your English is genuine or not. Therefore, when you practice, you can do your best to imitate and play music in particular styles.

And moreover, still, it is inevitable that you are highly encouraged to listen to traditional Blues music as contemporary Blues music mostly have many other blended characteristics which are meant to produce more colors in Blues music, it is not easy to identify obvious differences between Blues and regular popular music sometimes. This then makes the process of identifying essences of Blues music uneasy upon learning.

Below I have found representing music works which are of more traditional Blues via Youtube. You can listen to these available music instantly. Please also pay attention to certain common and different parts among these music.

Robert Johnson: John Lee Hooker: Muddy Water:

BB King:

Buddy Guy:

Albert Lee:

Stevie Ray Vaughan:

After listening, do you feel anything special about Blues music ?

There are four elements in music: melody, harmony, rhythm and timbre. Thus, in order to find clear elements in Blues music, we will need to identify the main characteristics which can help us learn faster. However, you also need to know that, in order to play different authentic 'tastes' of the song style, time is needed for you to be immersed and bathed in that particular type of music. It's just like for the best learning in a new language you will need to be exposed to the language for a good long time.

Therefore, if you are serious about playing Blues well, please listen to Blues music continuously or even to hum along to it. Then slowly, you will get to know how to allow your Blues music to be more authentic after learning all these elements. Among the four elements, besides "timbre" is relevant to the use of musical instruments, the other three elements are what we need to analyze and learn musically.

◇ Blues Chords （Harmony）

The basic chord form of Blues is a chord structure which mainly features a dominant seventh chord, and chord series used are I , IV , V series within one key.

Therefore the basic chords are:

I 7   IV7   V 7

Taking A key as one example, it is like:

Taking E key as one example:

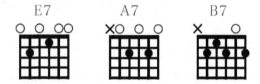

◈ Form of Blues Music

Blues music contain a basic 12 measure circular form , which is also called 'Blues 12 measure.' That is, after playing the 12th measure each time, you then will need to return to the 1st measure and continue playing. With an addition of the previous Blues chord, the basic form of Blues is as below:

I_7	(IV_7)	(I_7)	
IV_7		I_7	
V_7	IV_7	I_7	(V_7)

And certainly the 12-measure form is not an absolute form. We can also hear that even it is more traditional Blues, it is very easy to have variations in form.

◇ Blues Rhythm

The basic Blues rhythm is Shuffle rhythm and that is among a triple in one beat count, taking off rhythm of the 2nd note.

For convenient production and reading purposes in sheet music, it is often presented with two eighth notes and marked as below:

$$(\; \sqcap = \; \overset{3}{\sqcap} \;)$$

Attention please, although rest signs are being taken off from the mark, we still play the music as if the rest signs are still being played. Therefore, you will hear that it doesn't sound like the notes are all grouped together, instead, it sounds like the notes are being cut off and produces a bouncy feeling (staccato). And we will use this way to show all sheet music demonstrations in later sections.

On guitar, this rhythm is often played as:

| ↓ ↑ | ↓ ↑ | ↓ ↑ | ↓ ↑ |

Therefore, for basic Blues playing, taking A key as one example, below is your example:

A7	(D7)	(A7)	
D7		A7	
E7	D7	A7	(E7)

◈ Often Used Keys of Fingerstyle Blues

As you need to play bass section upon a solo time, thus if the root of a chord is an open note, it then will be very easy for you to play. Root of chord notes of A7 D7 E7 in A key happen to be the open notes of the 5th, 4th and 6th strings. Therefore, Blues in A key is the most often played key on the guitar; and among E7 A7 B7 of E key, it is only the root note of B7 is not an open note and you will need to rely on your left hand fingers to press the B root note. However, as it's a V series chord, it doesn't appear very frequent in Blues 12 measure. Therefore E key Blues is also one of the easiest keys for the guitar to elaborate.

We have played basic progressions in previous A key Blues, next let's play an E key Blues 12 measure!

Track
2

E7	(A7)	(E7)		
A7		E7		
B7	A7	E7	(B7)	

◈ Blues Notes

A basic musical scale of Blues is developed with a minor pentatonic scale, and Blues notes in Blues is thus an addition $^{\#}4$ ($^{b}5$) in a minor pentatonic scale giving a very vicissitudinous feeling of Blues music.

【Minor Pentatonic Scale Format : 1　^{b}3　4　5　^{b}7】

A Key : A　C　D　E　G

E Key : E　G　A　B　D

【Blues Scale Format：1 ♭3 4 #4 5 ♭7】

A Key：A C D D# E G

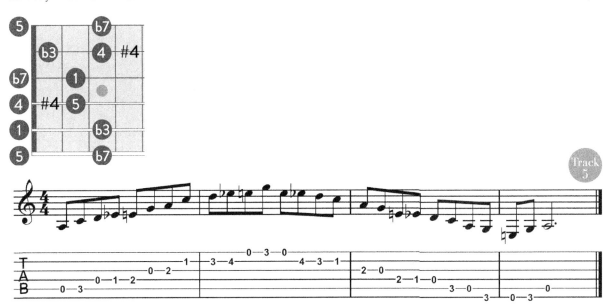

E Key：E G A A# B D

【12 Measure Practice】

When playing Blues melody practices in the beginning, you may follow background rhythm to play a triplet or use Shuffle rhythm as the rhythm of melody.

For example:

A Key /

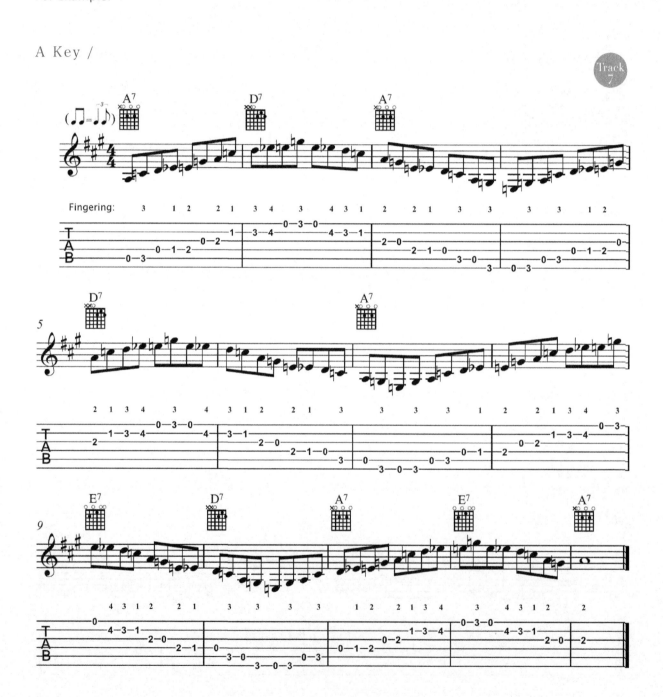

E Key /

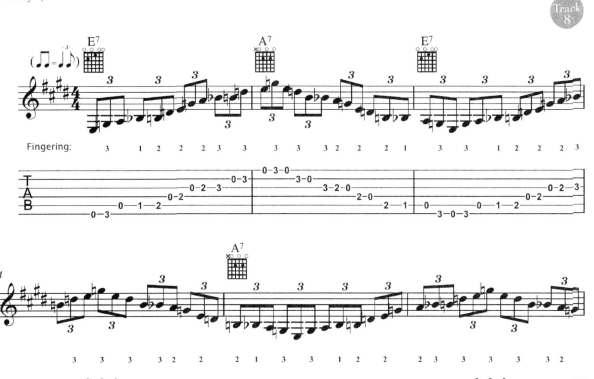

Fingering:

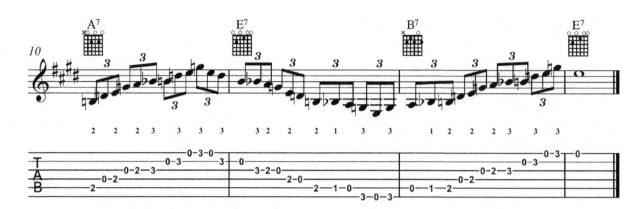

Please pay special attentions to the entire feeling of how the music sounds like when playing #4 in Blues notes.

【Adding Melodic Practices】

A Key /

Demo I

Track 9

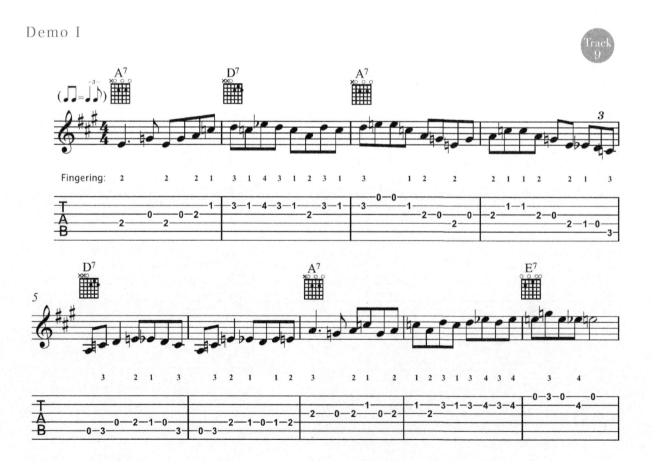

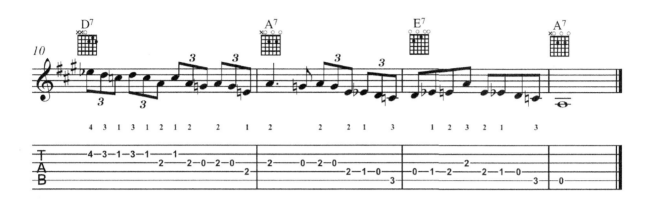

Demo II

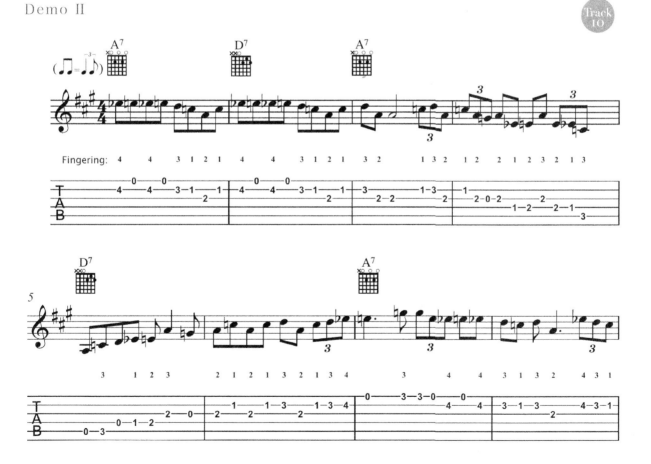

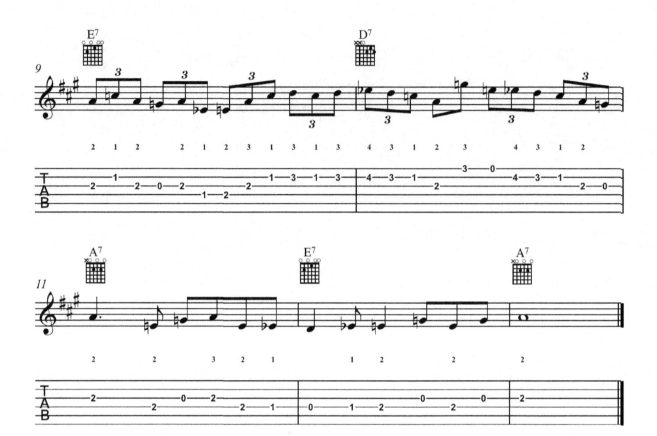

E Key /

Demo I

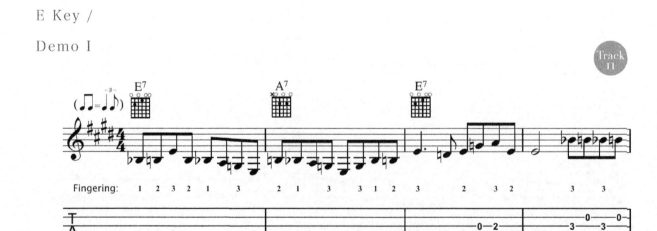

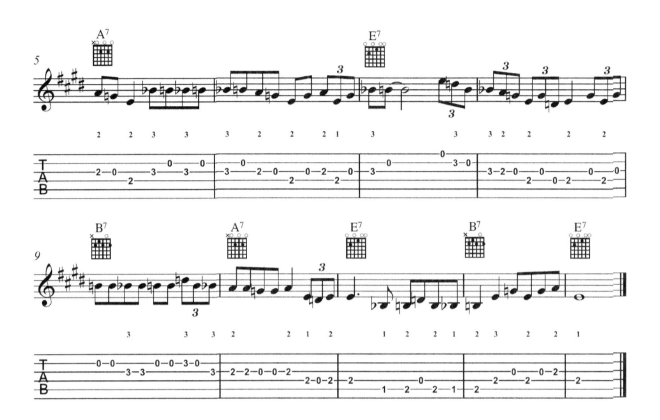

Demo II

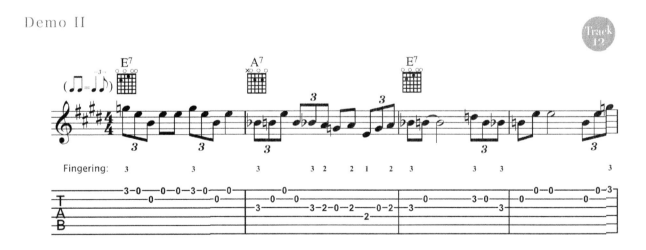

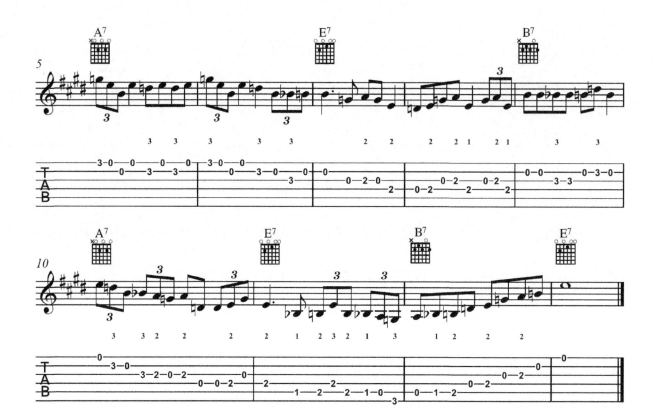

◈ Expressions of Blues

If the above playing sounds like the a robotic and dull Blues melodies, that simply means Blues isn't authentic enough. It simply just something sounds like Blues.

Different musical styles have different expressions and frequently used expressions or ornaments of Blues on a guitar are often being demonstrated with bending, sliding, hammer-ons and pull-offs. I believe that all these left hand techniques are already being mastered by many of you; however, Blues music can be deeply affected by timing of appearance or positions of beat, and this is where we need to learn about and I would like to invite you to imitate.

【Bending】

Bending is the most often seen and used technique of Blues on a guitar. However, bending is relatively difficult to perform on a acoustic guitar. It is often used with softer string quality or an electric guitar which allows players to bend strings more easily. If you really want to use bending on a acoustic guitar, a powerful finger strength is often required, and please be careful not to break the strings, or you can use a guitar that has a shorter neck.

A Key /

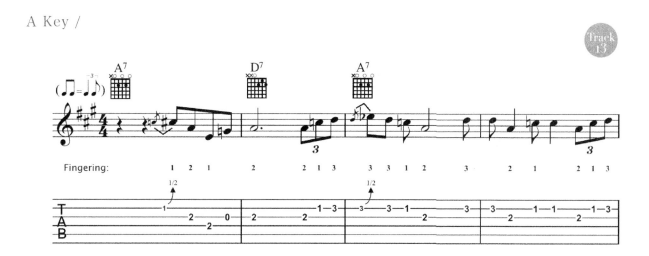

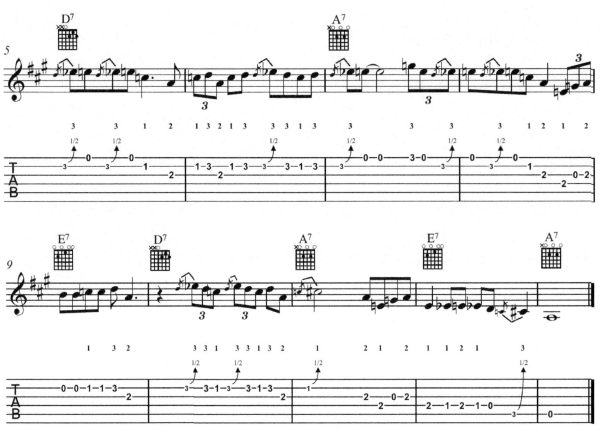

E Key /

Track 14

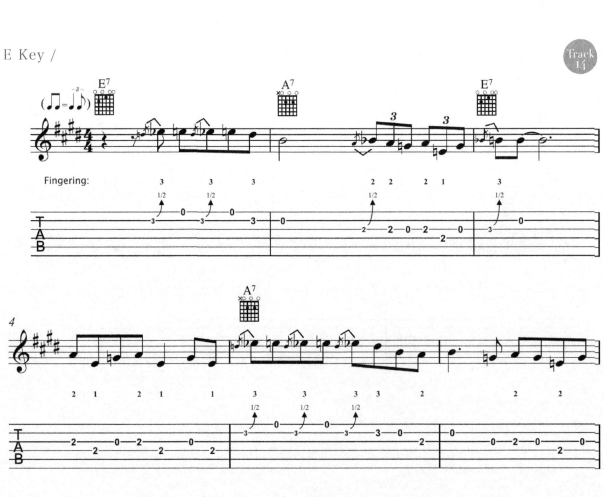

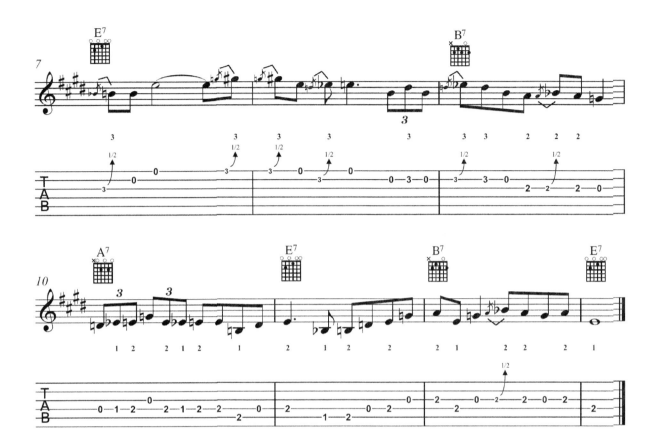

【Sliding】

As bending technique can be very challenging to be executed on a acoustic guitar, a technique which produces quite a similar effect-'sliding' then is often being used to imitate effects of a bending technique. And certainly, the features of 'sliding' itself are very suitable for uses and ornaments of changing fingering positions.

A Key /

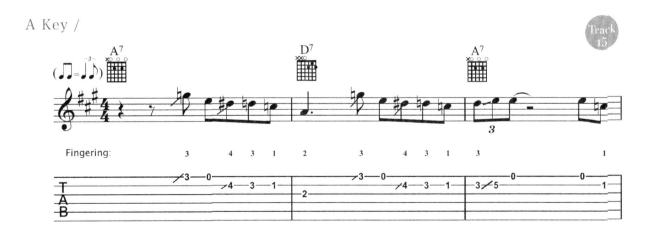

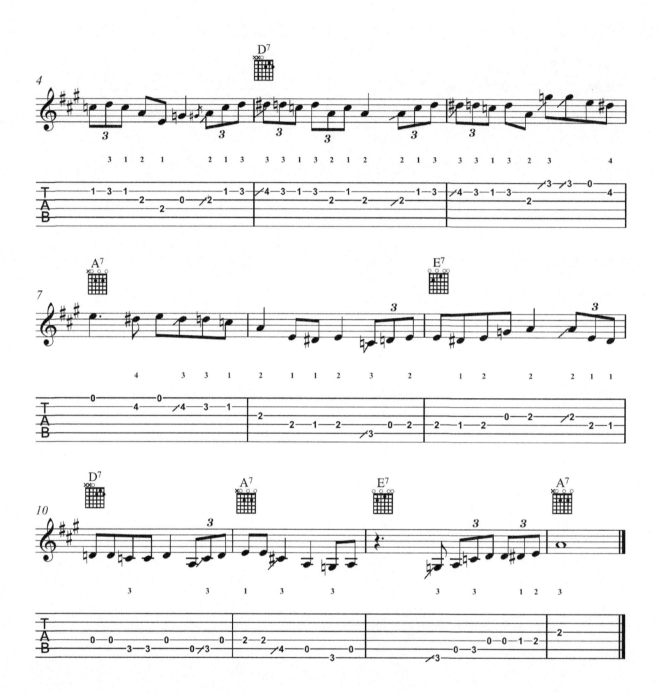

E Key /

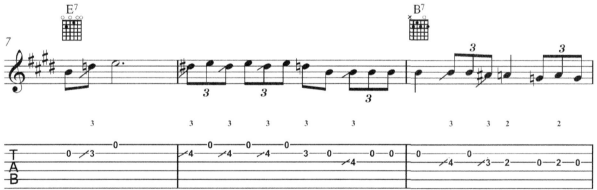

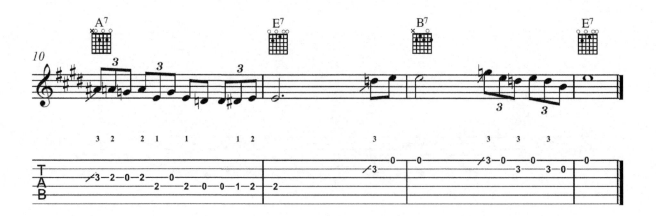

【Hammer-Ons】

Expressions produced by the of 'Hammer-Ons' technique is even more different. It can easily show a feeling of bouncy and an exciting emotions. Normally speaking, there will be more obvious use in faster Blues music. And certainly light hammering will also produce a smooth and soothing effect whereas continuous hammer-ons will sound even smoother than a melody produced by direct string-plucking.

A Key /

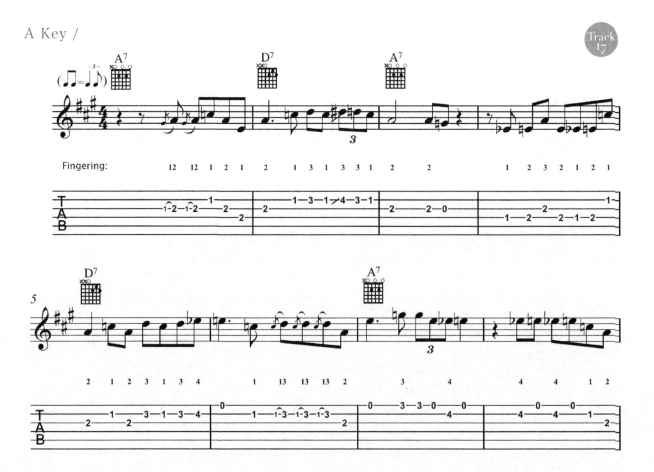

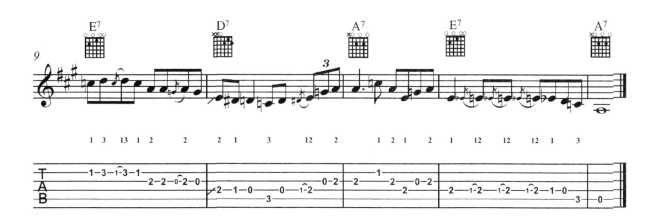

E Key /

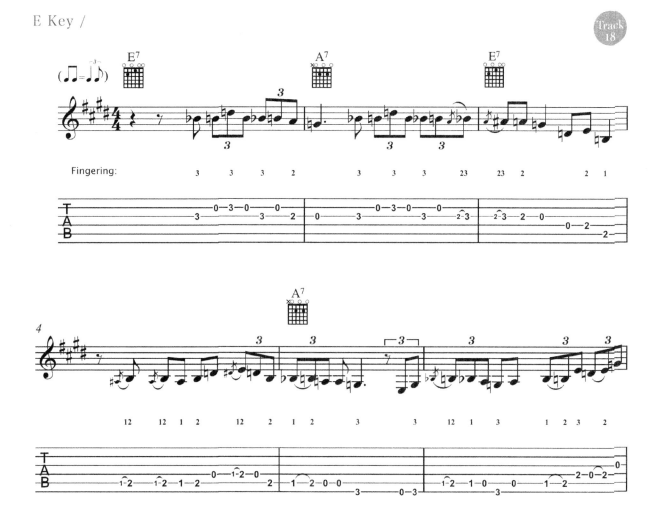

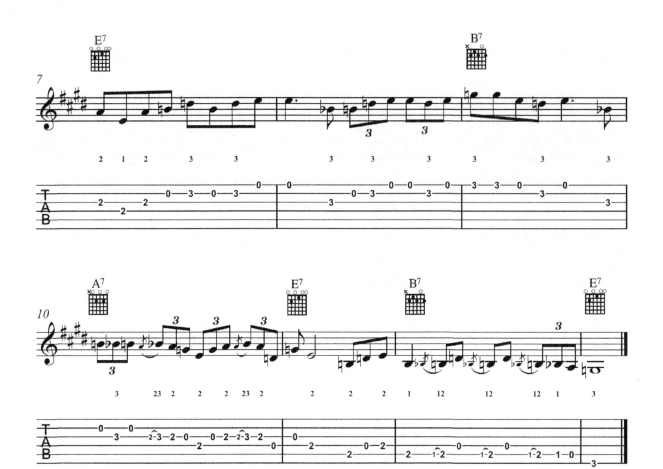

【Pull-Offs】

Pulling-off technique produces very similar expressions to that produced by hammer-ons, however, it is just of the contrary direction. Hammer-ons is conducted from low notes to high notes; whereas pull-offs is from high notes to low notes. Therefore, these two techniques are often being used continuously together and it is the so-called 'legato'.

A Key /

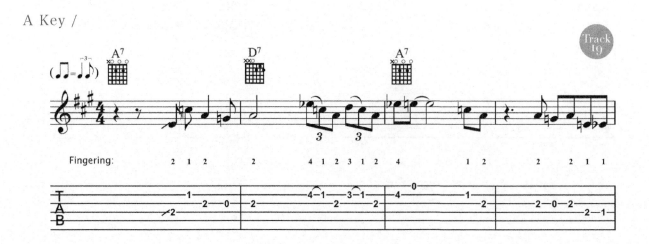

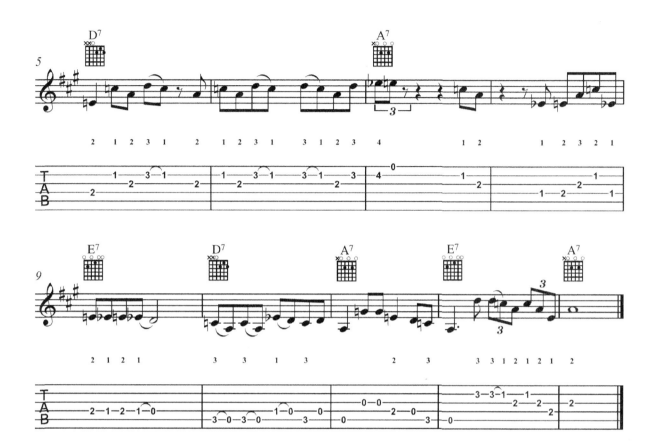

E Key /

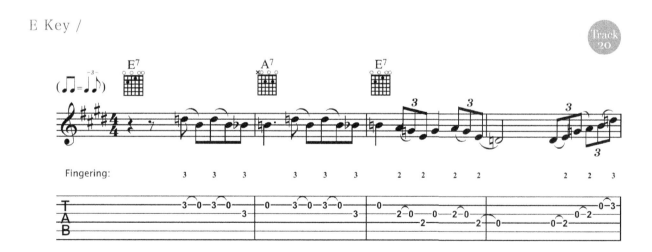

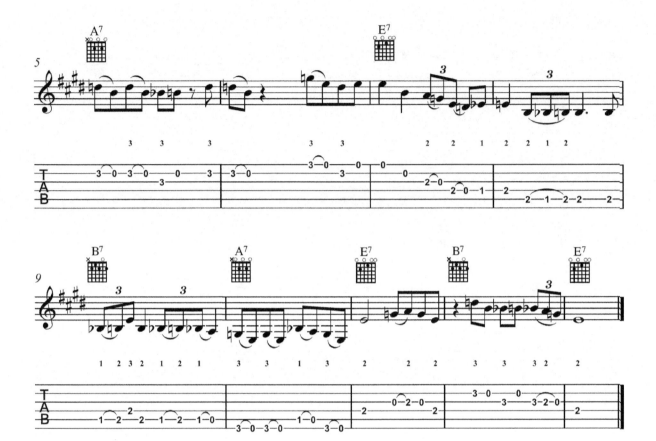

Etudes

Now let's integrate what we have learned previously and play one Blues etude!

A Key /

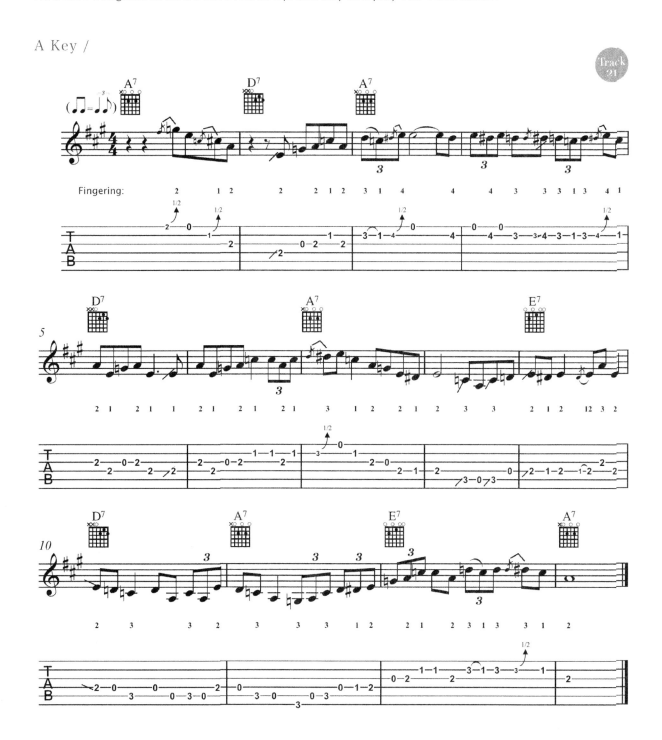

E Key /

Fingering:

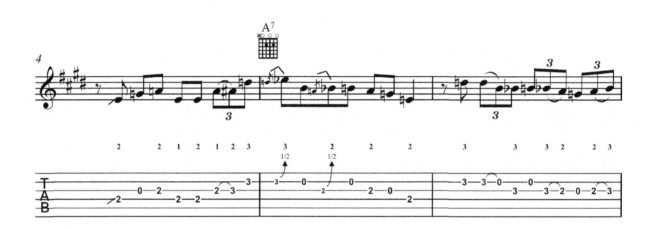

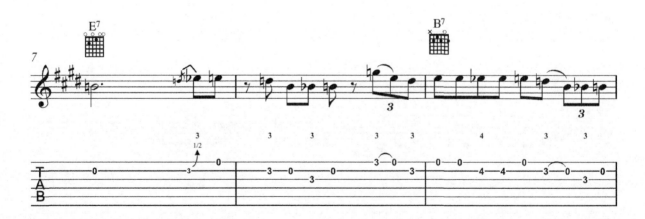

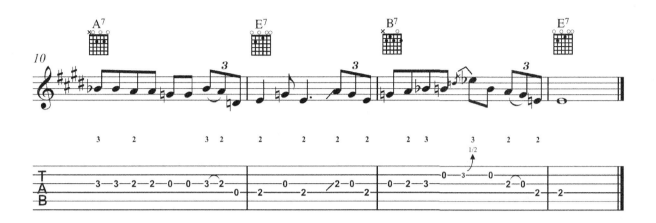

⟩ An AWESOME way to MEMORIZE and PRACTICE scale, note Position on Guitar !!

⟩ PRIVATE SECRET Theory combines **INTERVALs, CHORDs, ARPEGGIOs, MODEs** and HOW TO Practice to let you play Freely!!

⟩ 38 GREAT Examples & LICKS to Enhance your playing Technique & Scale Graphic MEMORIZING!!

This handbook let you memorize notes/scales position efficiently by using the best memory technique **"Image Memory Method"** !!

★ Amazon/iBook/GooglePlay/Kobo/Scribd/B&N/...

◈ Fingerstyle Playing Practice

Personally, I think playing our own Blues music alone allows us to express blues emotions even better! Therefore, I feel Blues is quite suitable for playing fingerstyle performances.
As I mentioned in my previous publication **"Playing Guitar So Easy-The Ultimate Book For Beginner"**, the easiest form of fingerstyle performance is a two-voice song performance, simply put, two-voice performance on guitar is melodic lines plus a root note. Therefore, we can just use Blues basics learned above to play simple two-voice Blues fingerstyle!

A Key /

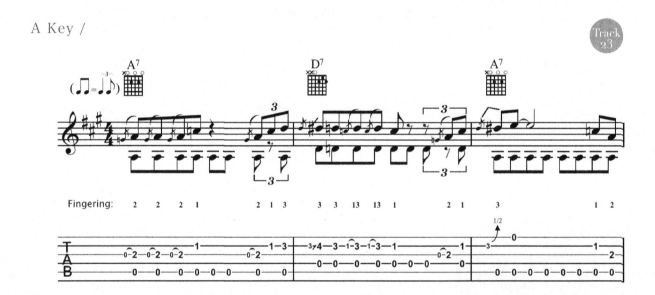

E Key /

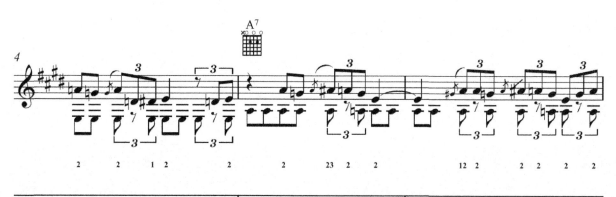

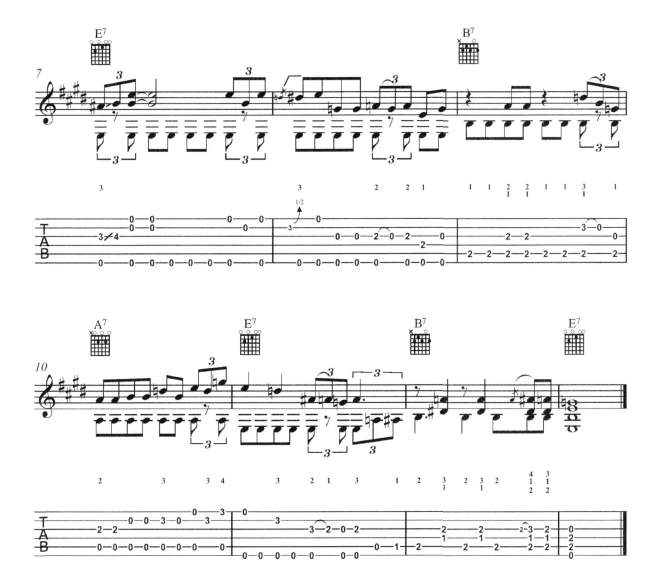

Solo
Fingerstyle

Blues
Guitar

Utilizing open note and inversion chord
allows us to have more fluent melodic
progressions when playing music, and
aurally to generate different acoustics.

Chapter TWO

Enriching Your Blues Playing

◈ Various Styles of Blues Rhythm

If classifying musical feelings of tempo for Blues rhythm, in addition to the most basic 'Shuffle' previously, there are still approximately four types basic tempo:

【Straight-four】

This is to turn the original one long and one short eighth note in Shuffle to a regular eighth note which is evenly distributed on the beat of an eighth note. That is, it is like a rhythm in which there is no dotted eighth notes in regular music.

In the two-voice performance demo below, we add **thumb-slap technique** of guitar to increase rhythmic feelings of this type. If you are not familiar with the thumb-slap technique, you may try to play it slowly or refer to the thumb-slap practice in a regular method book.

A Key /

E Key /

Fingering:

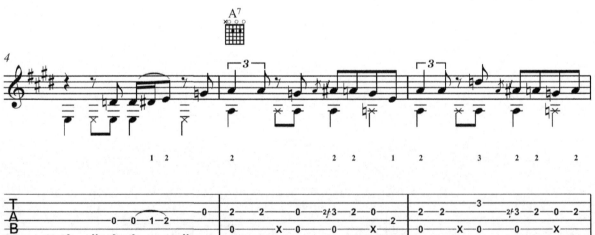

【12/8】

Rhythm has a time signature of 12/8 is to count a quaver as one beat, and the length of one measure equals to 12 beats. This tempo often shows in slow tempo (or 'Adagio') Blues music. And you may treat this as the original 4/4 time, but each beat would feel like a triplet consisting of quaver note.

A Key /

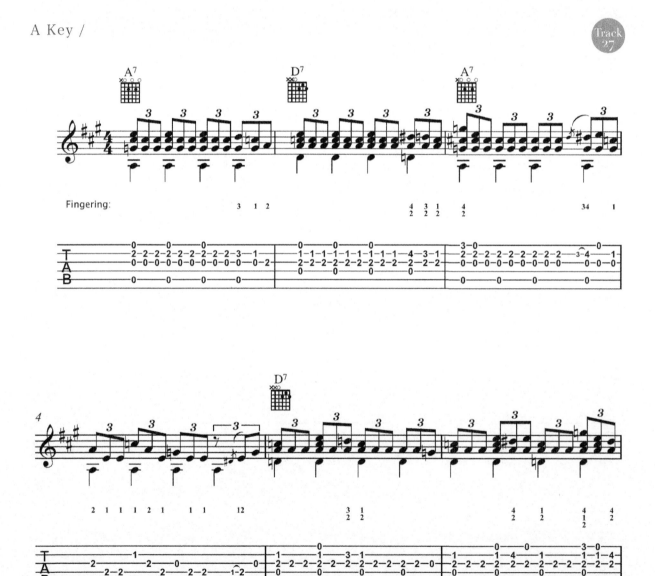

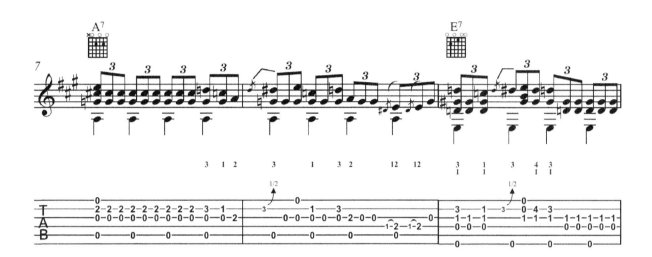

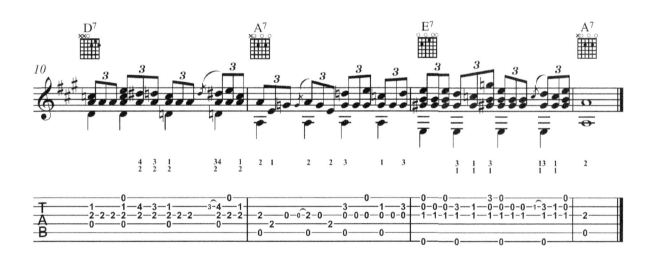

E Key /

Fingering:

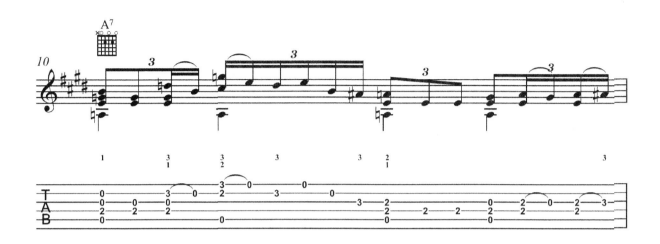

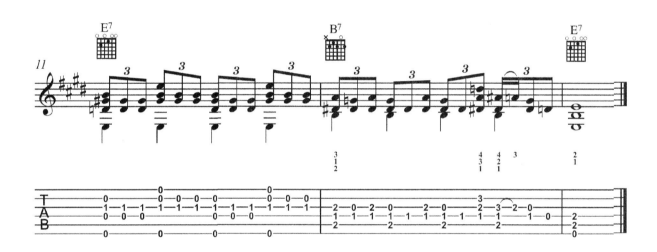

【Two-beat】

That is a two-beat rhythm. This type of rhythmic system actually originates from the fast tempo (allegro) in Jazz music. Although the time signature is written as 44, it follows bass voice rhythmic pattern to count 1-2-1-2. Therefore, it is the fast tempo (allegro) songs that uses this type of rhythm in Blues music.

A Key /

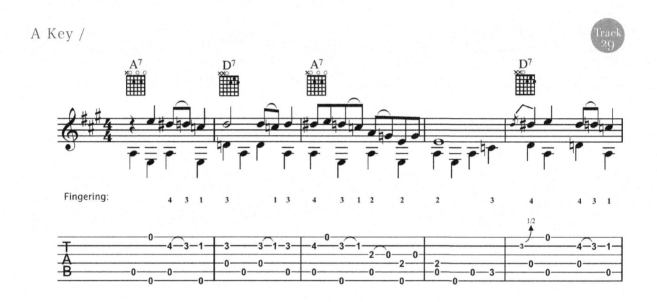

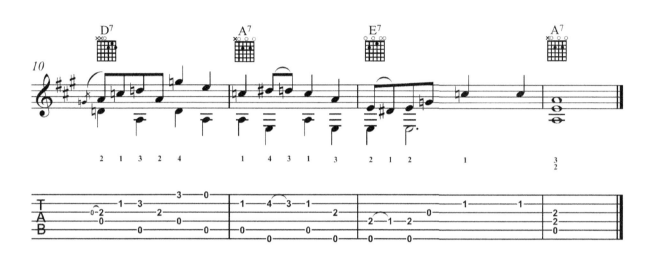

E Key /

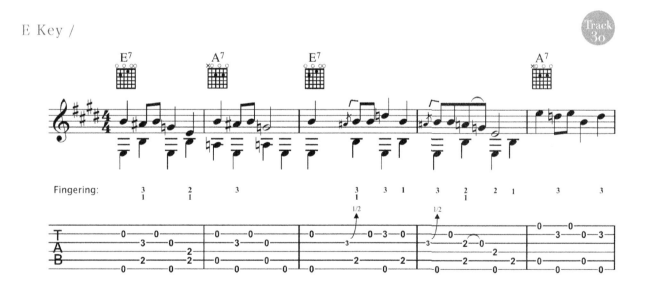

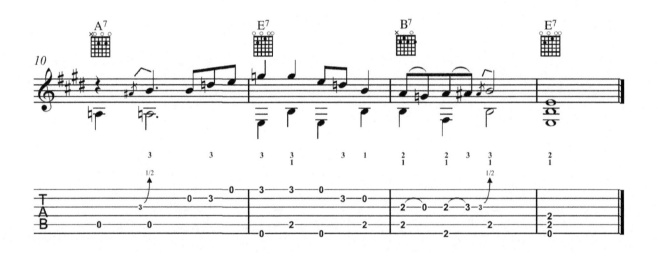

【16 feel 】

This is about using sixteenth notes as the rhythm. This allows Blues music to produce a funky, up-beat speed of music mostly appears on Moderato (medium speed).

A Key /

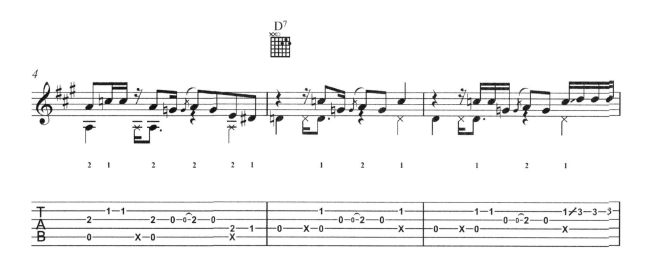

E Key /

Fingering:

◈ Applications on Open Note

Utilizing open note allows us to have more fluent melodic progressions when playing music, and aurally to generate different acoustics. The playings of fingerstyle guitar usually will need to include high, medium and bass voices. Therefore, using open notes is a very good method. It is just like we often choose A key and E key to play Blues so we can fulfill such considerations.

In a regular guitar tuning method, the open notes are: E B G D A E. We can see how they can be used upon playing.

< When in A key > ：

A7

Taking A7 chord of I series as an example, the 5th string A is a root note and D of the 4th string is the 4th note; whereas the 3rd string G is ^{b}7th note. The 2nd string is 9th (2nd) note and the 1st string E is the 5th note. Therefore, when playing the first chord A7, **open notes of the 1st, 2nd and 3rd strings can be used**, and as the 4th string D is the 4th note, there is relatively more limitations upon application.

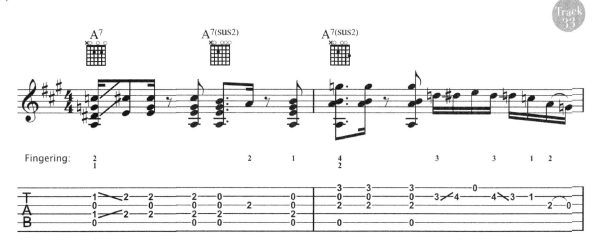

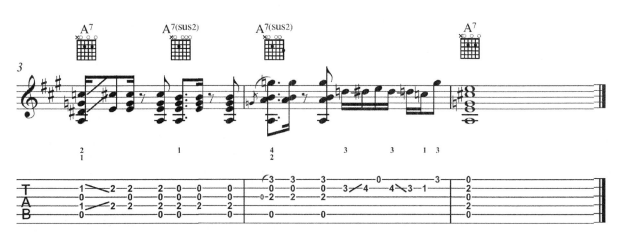

D7

Taking D7 chord of IV series, the 4th string D is a root note, the 3rd string G is a 4th note, the 2nd string B is the 6th note, the 1st string E is a 9th (2nd)note. Therefore, when playing the 2nd chord D7, **open notes of the 1st, 2nd strings can be applied**. As the 3rd string G is a 4th note, then there is relatively more limitations upon use.

E7

Taking E7 chord of V series as one example; E of the 6th string is root, A of the 5th string is the 4th note; D of the 4th string is ♭7th note; G of the 3rd string is ♭3rd note; B of the 2nd string is 5th note; E of the 1st string is root note. Therefore, when playing E7 of the 3rd chord, **open notes of the 1st, 2nd and 4th strings can be applied**. As A of the 5th string A is a 4th note, and the 3rd string G is a ♭3rd note, therefore there is more limitations upon application.

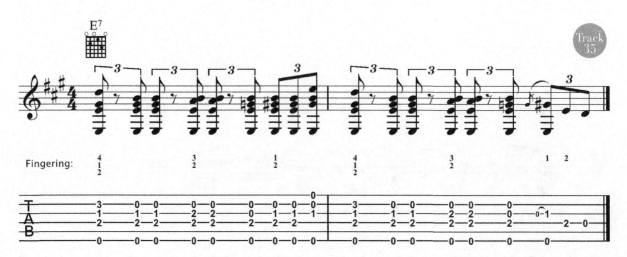

Etudes

The addition of open note often enables us to do a big scale of position change upon playing. You are highly encouraged to try this upon your practice times.

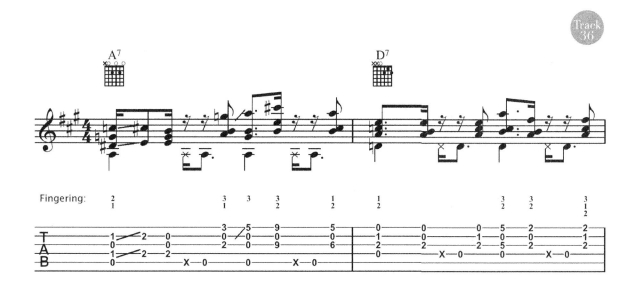

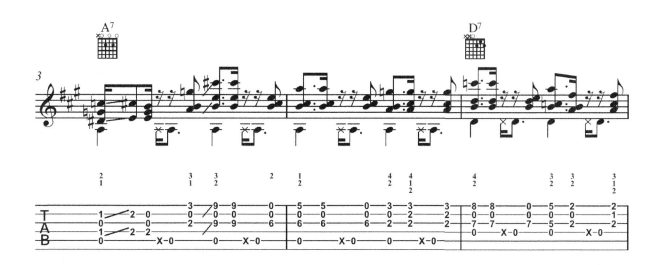

< When in E Key > :

B7

Taking B7 chord of V series as one example, the B which must be pressed at the 5th string is a root note, the 4th string D is ♭3rd note, the 3rd string G is ♭6th note, the 2nd string B is a root note, the 1st string E is the 4th note. Therefore, when playing the 3rd chord B7, only open notes of the 2nd string can be applied; whereas other strings have relatively more limitations upon application.

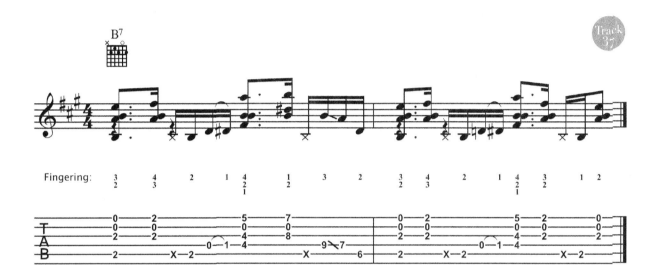

Etudes

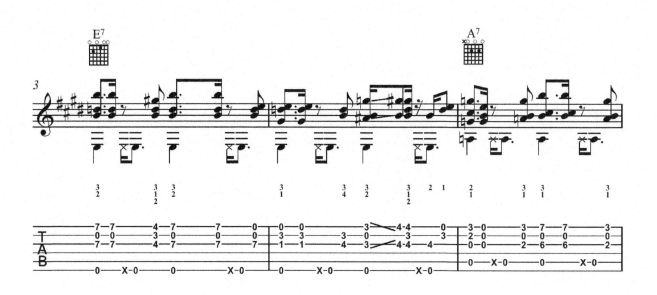

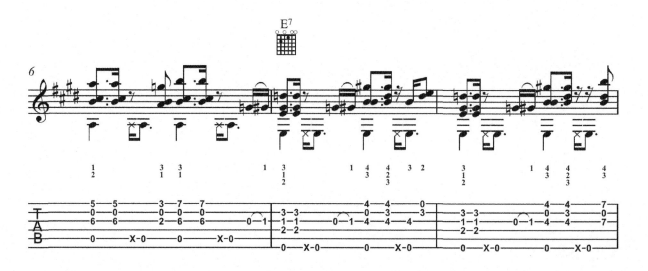

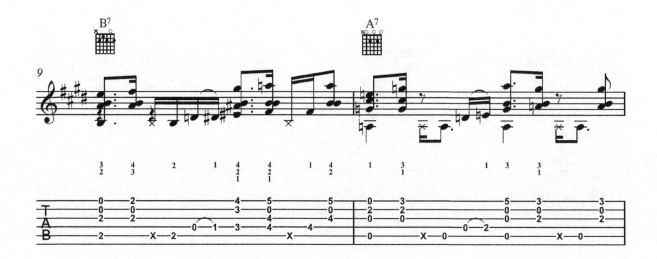

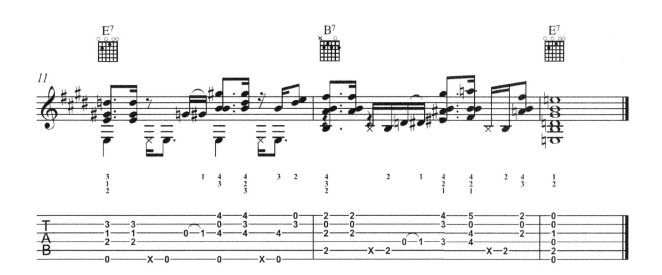

⟩ Designed for most kinds of guitar BEGINNERS

⟩ Only EASY playing, no hard theory

⟩ Quickly learn the BASICs that you need

⟩ 108 mp3s of Examples for downloading !!

⟩ 3 MAIN DIRECTIONS:

Song Melody, Accompaniment, Fingerstyle Playing on guitar in a Simple Way.

★Amazon/iBook/GooglePlay/Kobo/Scribd/B&N/....

◈ Applications on Inversion Chord

An inversion chord uses the lowest note (or root) and replace it with other composing note as the lowest note. In addition to an open note which allows us to play with more position changes, it, particularly to a low voice section, can even produce bass voice melodic lines other than single note progressions. And certainly, an open note can increase different acoustic effects so for the same chord progression, it would be less tedious. For more uses on inversion chords and descriptions, please refer to my another book: "**Your Training Notebook on Pop Music Special Chord Progressions**".

【Root and Inversion Positions of A7】

1- root, 3- triad, 5- 5th note , b7- 7th note

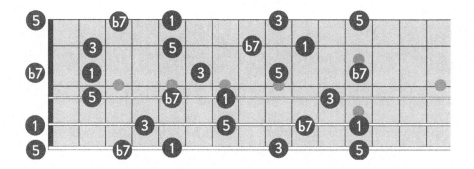

The 3rd of the chord placed as the lowest note – 1st inversion
The 5th of the chord placed as the lowest note – 2nd inversion
The 7th of the chord placed as the lowest note – 3rd inversion

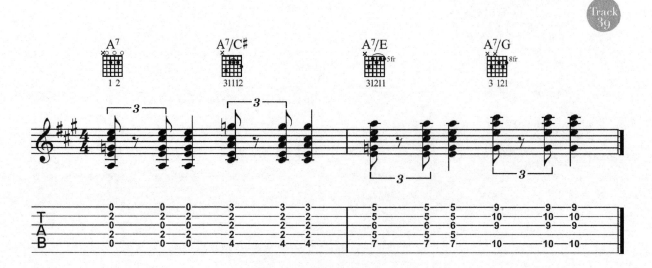

【Root and Inversion Positions of D7】

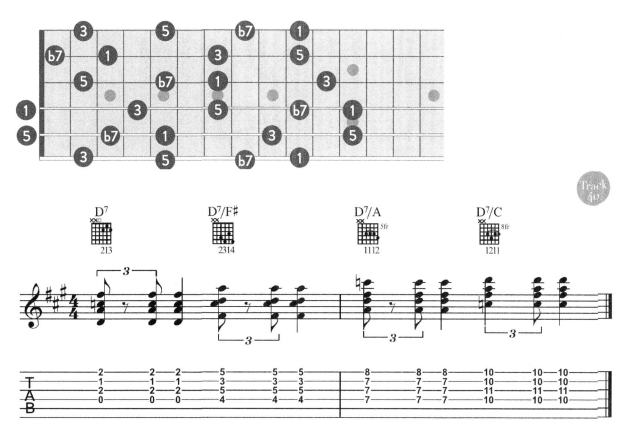

【Root and Inversion Positions of E7】

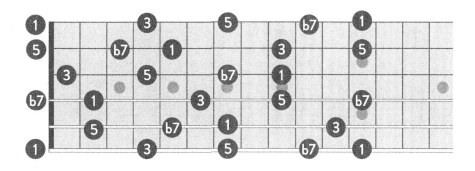

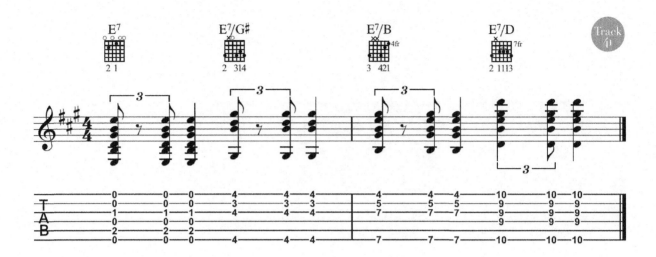

【Root and Inversion Positions of B7】

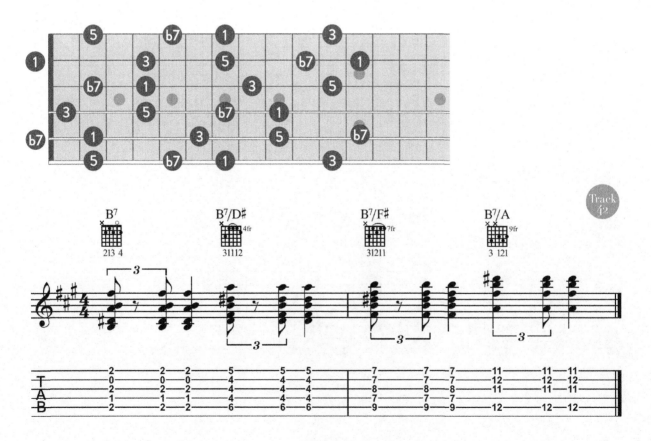

The above contents also represent respectively the fingerings of inversion chords when we place the lowest notes onto the 6th, 5th and 4th strings. Please remember to do additional practices according to the lowest notes placed on different strings of each individual chord.

A Key Etude

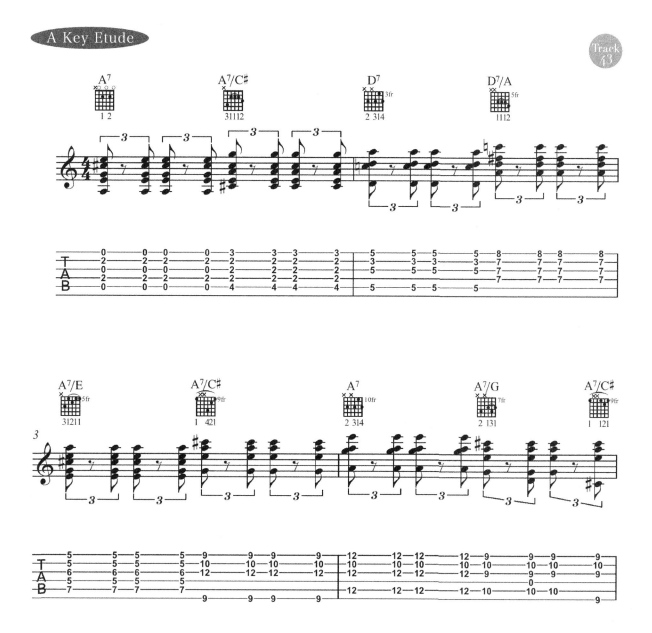

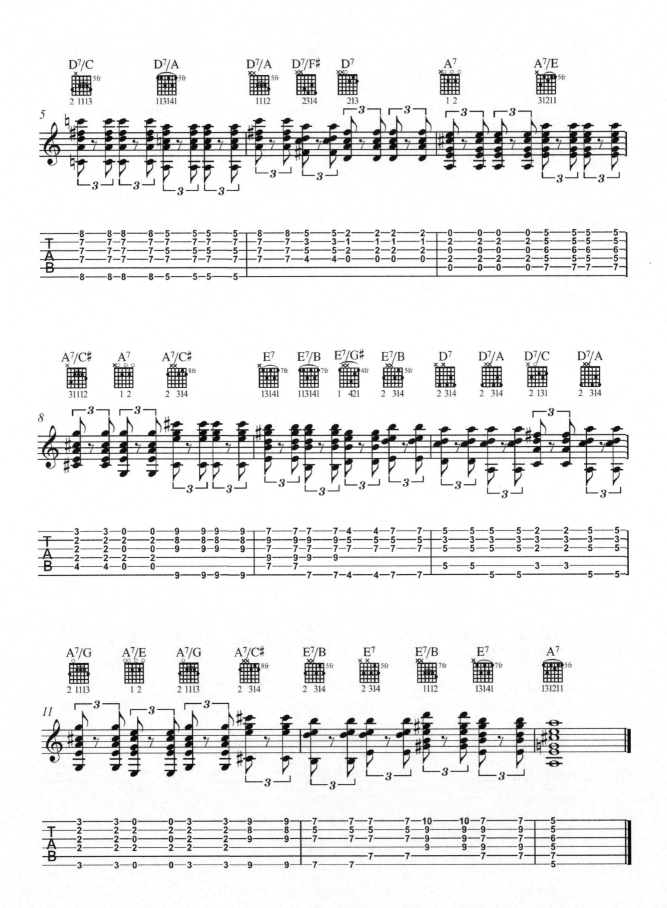

E Key Etude

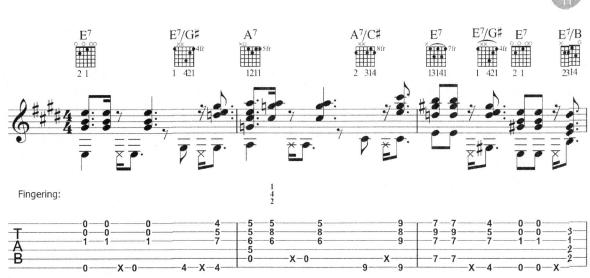

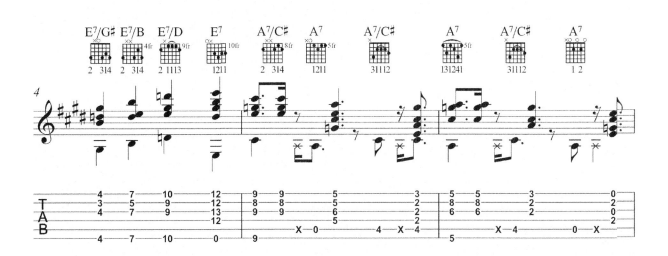

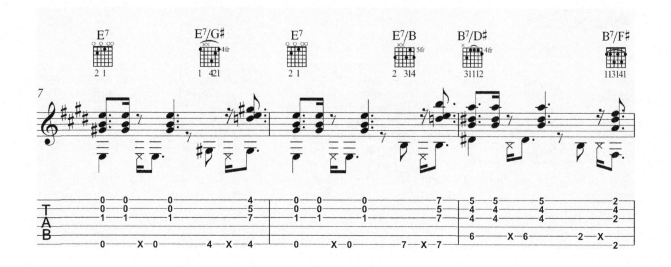

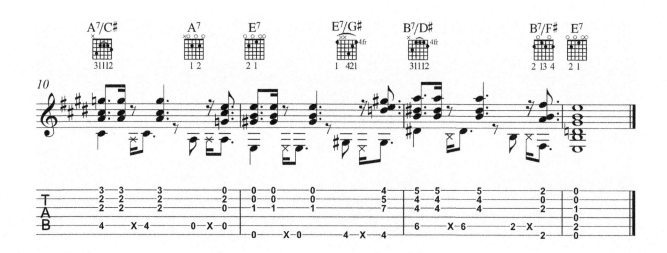

After you are able to play inversion chords, in the same time, this also means that you have learned the other playing positions of the SAME chord. That is the 5 fi ngering templates (C A G E D templates). For more discussions on fretboard positi ons, please refer to author's another publication: "**Fretboard Secret HandBook**".

◇ Accompaniment and Riffs

Comparing Blues music to other types of music, more often we play Blues riffs in sentences while singing and by doing so, you can enrich Blues feelings for the entire song. Many masters of Blues music can play and sing alone; therefore, if you can play the accompaniment with a guitar and add riffs on your own, you are not so far away from becoming a master.

In order to reach such step, you must become more familiar with Blues notes and positions of chords on a fretboard. And you also need to be able to play the same musical phrases of Blues on different positions.

Let's take the entire fretboard, divide it into 'chord' and 'scale' and then do a comparison.

< A Key > :

【A7 and A Blues Scale Fretboard Chart 】

1st is A7 chord root A.

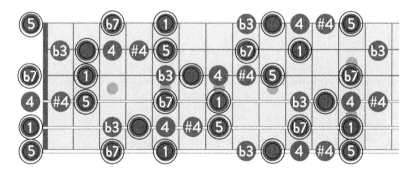

【D7 and A Blues Scale Fretboard Chart】

4th note is D7 chord root D.

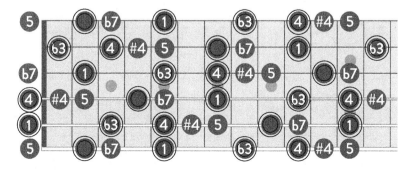

【E7 and A Blues scale fretboard chart】

5th note is E7 chord root E.

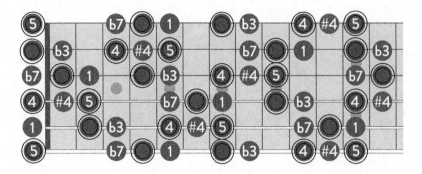

Etudes

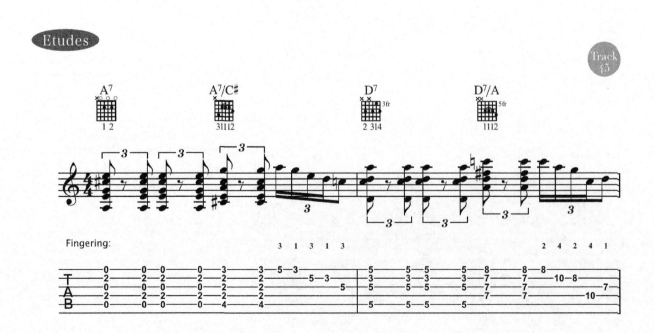

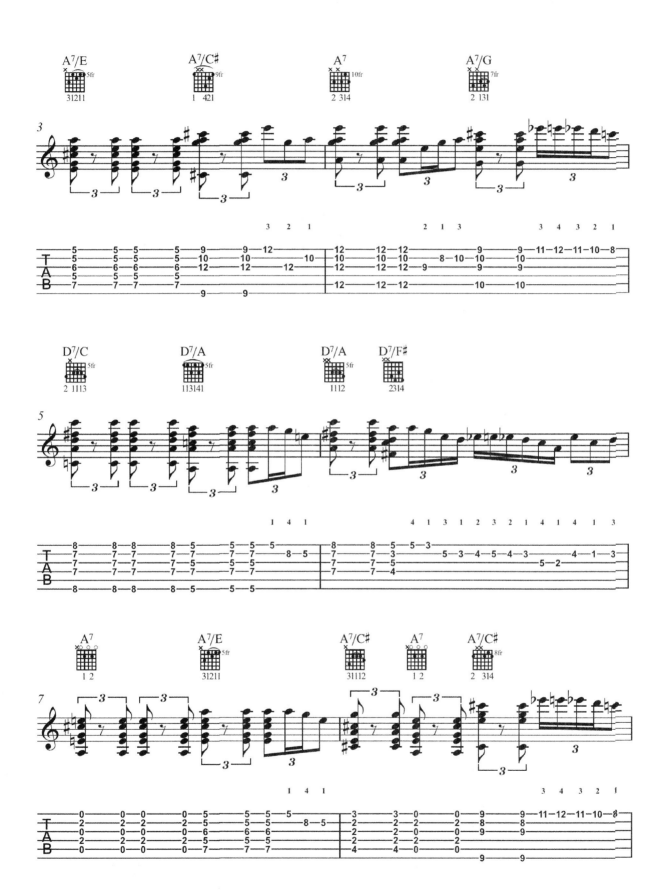

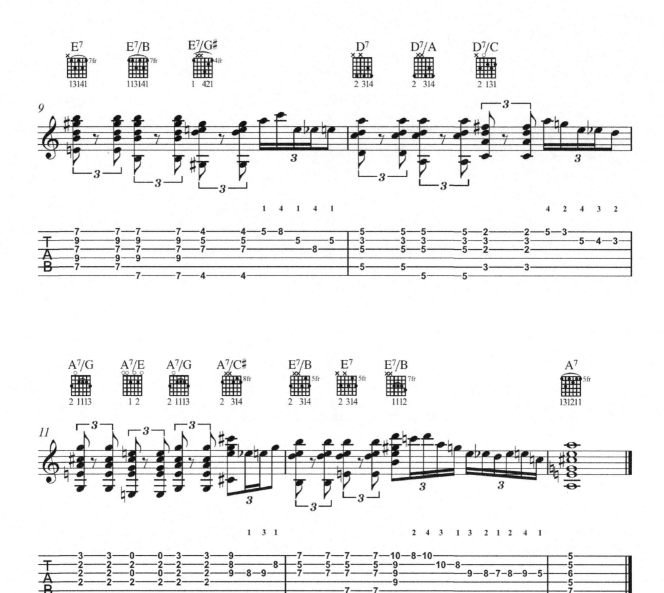

< E Key > ：

【E7 and E Blues Scale Fretboard Chart】

1st note is E7 chord root E.

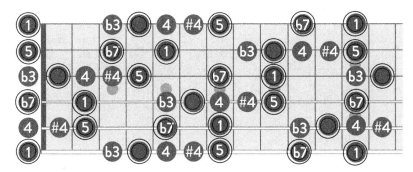

【A7 and E Blues Scale Fretboard Chart】

4th note is A7 chord root A.

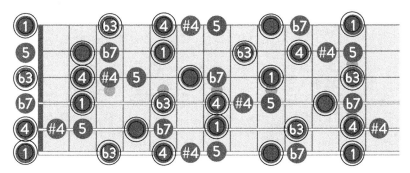

【B7 and E Blues Scale Fretboard Chart】

5th note is B7 chord root B.

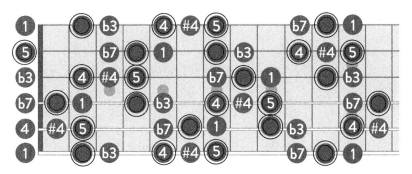

Etudes

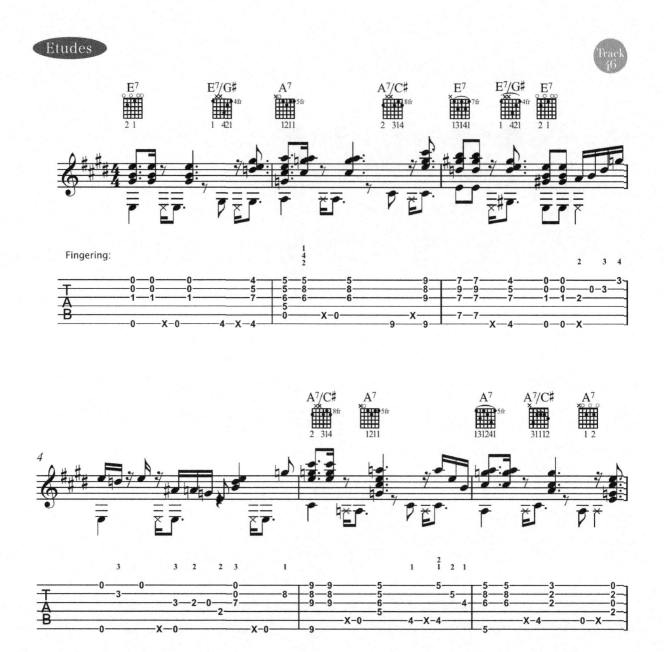

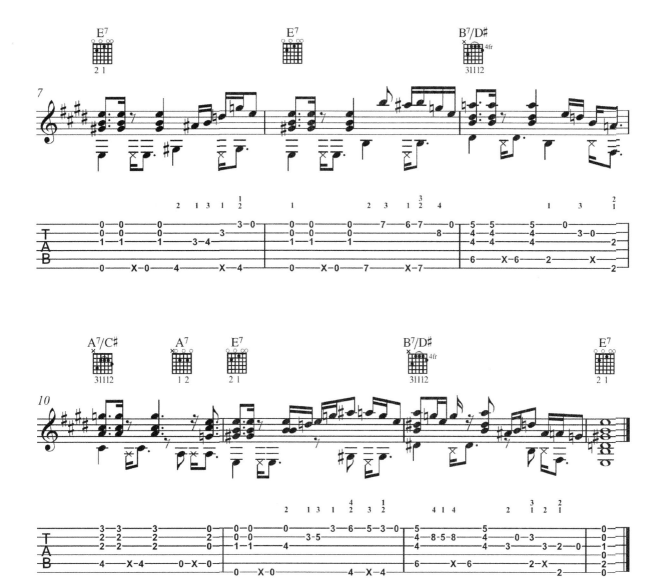

These two etudes are modified from some previous demo songs for a purpose of adding a riff. And for practicing scales on the same position, it is mostly based on chord positions while playing or positions of riff to playing the next chords. This thus helps you playing and singing more at ease. For more practice methods on chords and riff on fretboard, please refer to "**Fretboard Secret Handbook**".

◈ Integrated Performance Etudes

So are you familiar with previous etudes and concepts？ Then let's raise the level of difficulty a little more by adding previous techniques and chords, and see what happens…!

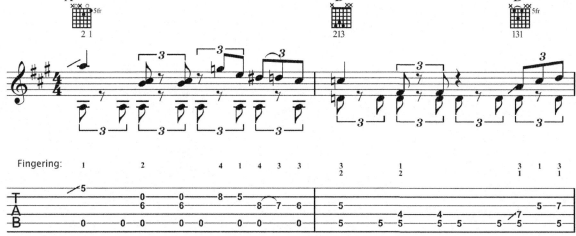

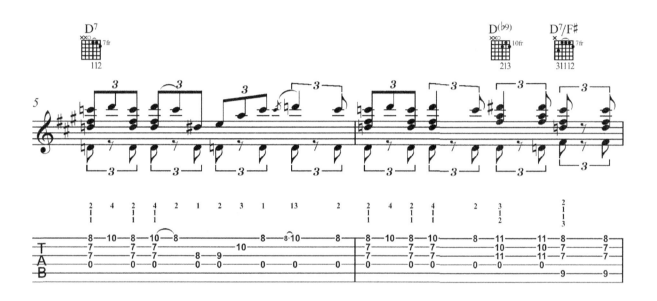

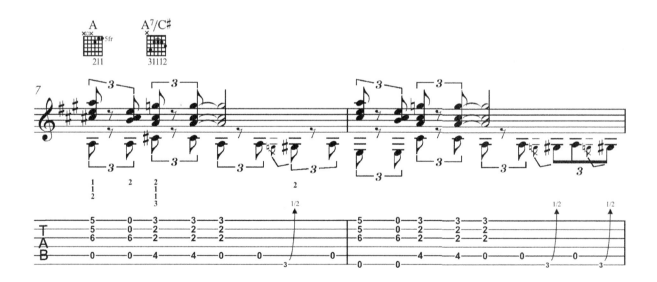

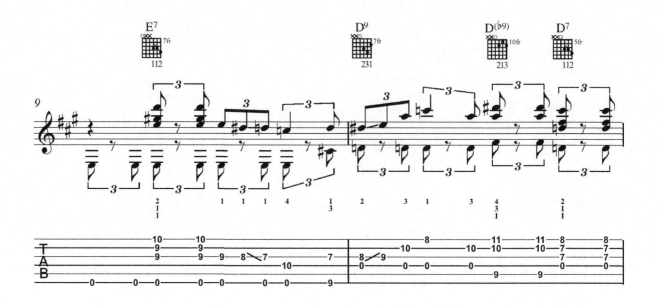

E Key Etude

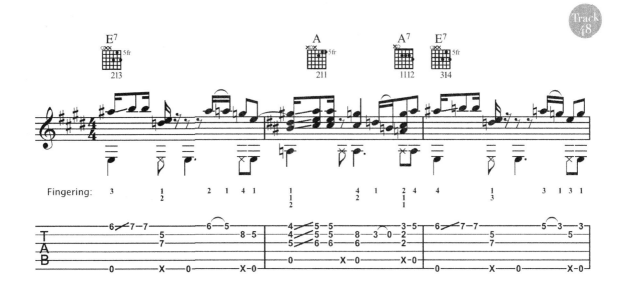

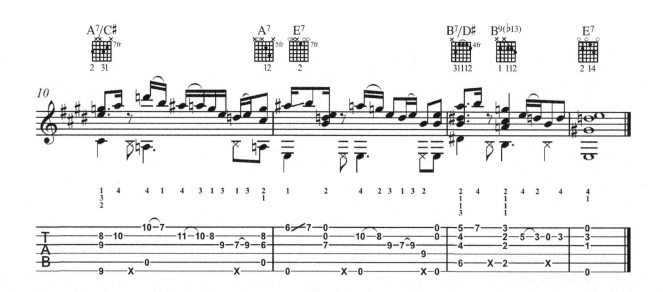

> **Carefully Selected Songs, Understand The Uniqueness**

Well-chosen 7 classic domestic and international pop music songs with unique chord progressions

> **Viewing From Pop Music Aspects, Easy To Learn And Use**

Complete sum-ups of harmony techniques in pop music applications and convenient to look-up upon compositions and arrangements.

> **Demonstrate Operation Flows, Clear At A Glance**

Step by step demonstrations from easy to complicated chord rearrangements, hands-on learning on harmony techniques.

★ Amazon/iBook/GooglePlay/Kobo/Scribd/B&N/.....

Solo Fingerstyle

Blues Guitar

This is why music is so magical! By simply
viewing this with musical notes, all the
musical notes can be fully used; however,
if you are aiming for playing good-sounding
and atmospheric music, it doesn't work by
directly playing all these musical notes.

Chapter THREE

Thinkings and Improvisations of

Advanced Blues

◈ Turnaround

Turnaround refers to a change in bridge for proceeding to the next circulation (repetition) in Blues music form in the very last one or two measures. This change has several particular patterns which are often used in Blues. Here is an approximate introduction:

【1st note and 5th note chromatic descending】

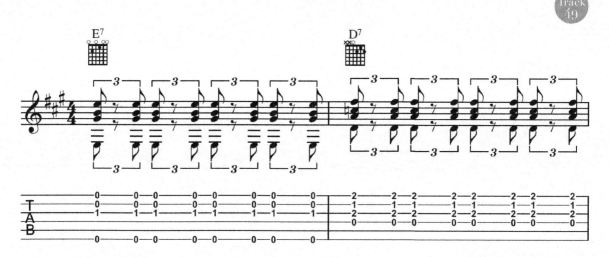

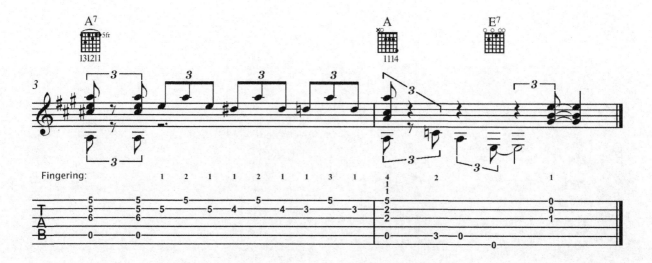

【5th note chromatic descending and ♭7th note chromatic descending（6th interval）】

【3rd note chromatic descending and 5th note chromatic descending（6th interval）】

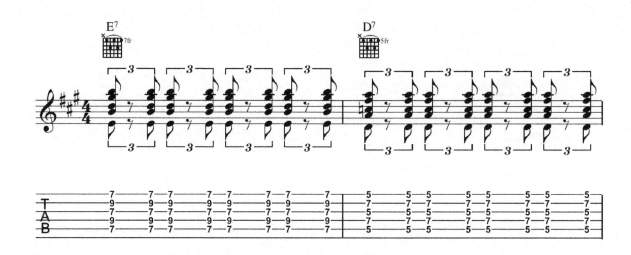

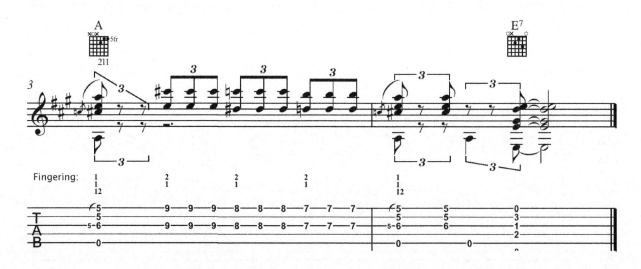

【1st note and ♭7th note chromatic descending】

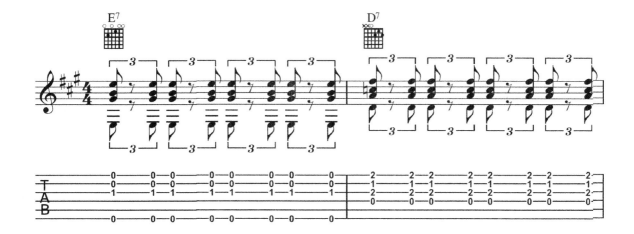

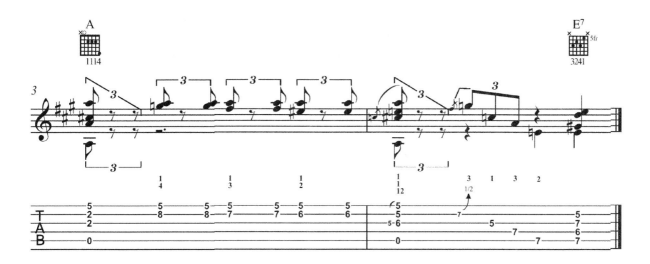

In addition to these, you can also listen to other Blues musicians more as to how they deal with musical phrases upon turnaround. And if you are very interested in playing Blues, you can also try to develop turnarounds with your own 'styles'!

◈ Blues in Minor Keys

Of the previously introduced basic Blues chords I 7, IV7, V 7, a major 3rd or a minor 7th chords are adopted. Blues in a minor key, however, adopts elements of a natural minor key by replacing these three chords into a minor 3rd and a minor 7th format. That is **I m7, IVm7, V m7 (or V 7)** , with an addition of the original Blues scale which is transformed from a minor pentatonic scale. Therefore, the entire feeling of music would sound more sad than the basic Blues.

Here we change the demo chords which are played previously into a minor 3rd chord and a minor 7th chord for you to experience, followed by a minor Blues solo performance. **Please also remember to spend your own time to practice individual inversion chords and position changes of minor 3rd and minor 7th chords.**

【A Minor Blues Demo】

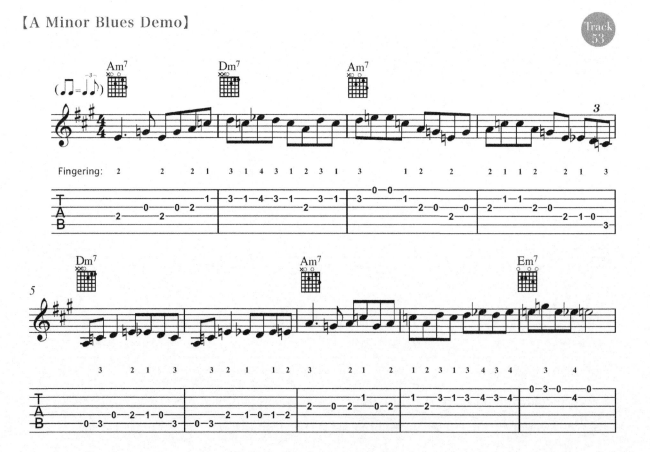

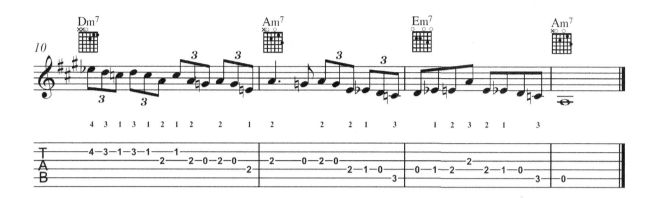

【A Minor Blues Fingerstyle Demo】

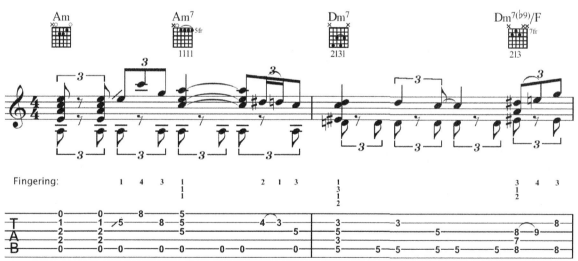

【E Minor Blues Demo】

【E Minor Blues Fingerstyle Demo】

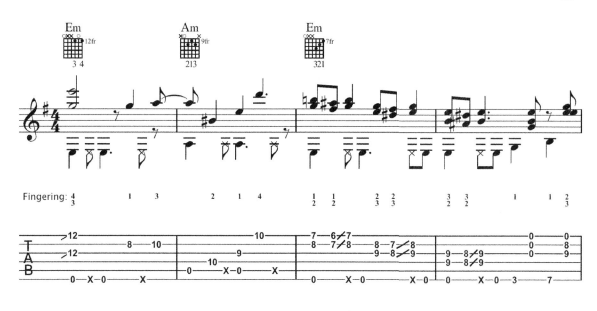

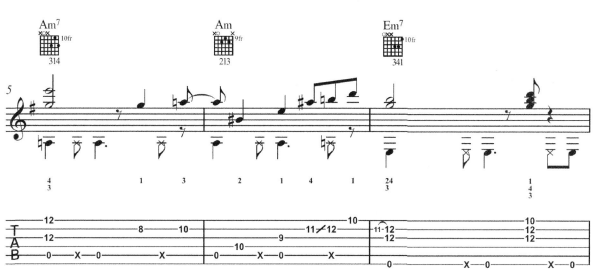

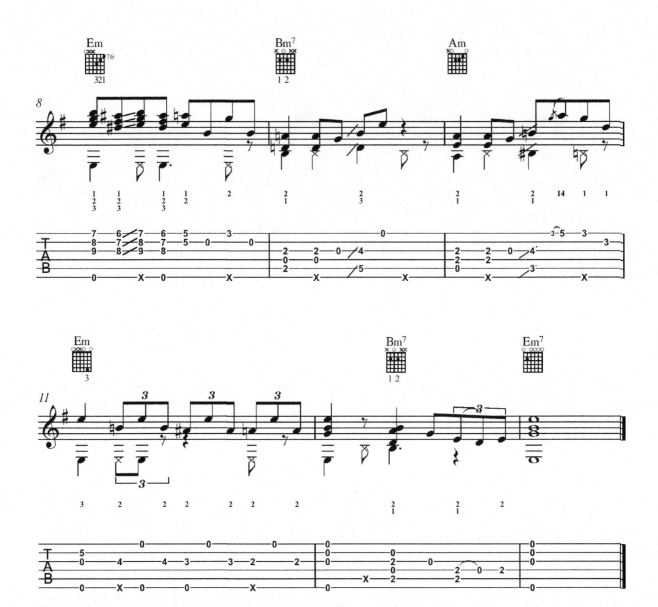

When practicing Blues in minor keys, you may also follow methods of the previous
Blues position practices on your own.

◈ Blues in Major Keys

For major Blues, chord speaking wise, the original basic major 3rd and minor 7th chords of Blues are still adopted. However, the basics of Blues scales have been changed to a major pentatonic scale, 1 2 3 5 6. And taking ♭3 as a Blues note, major Blues scale has become a 1 2 ♭3 3 5 6. And because of this, comparing to basic Blues music, major Blues gives a more delightful and energetic feeling.

Major Blues scale format：1 2 ♭3 3 5 6

A Key：A B C C# E F#

E Key：E F# G G# B C#

Here let's experience feelings presented by major key Blues scales. And next, we will also try to play some Blues solo etudes in major keys.

【A Major Blues Scale Demo】

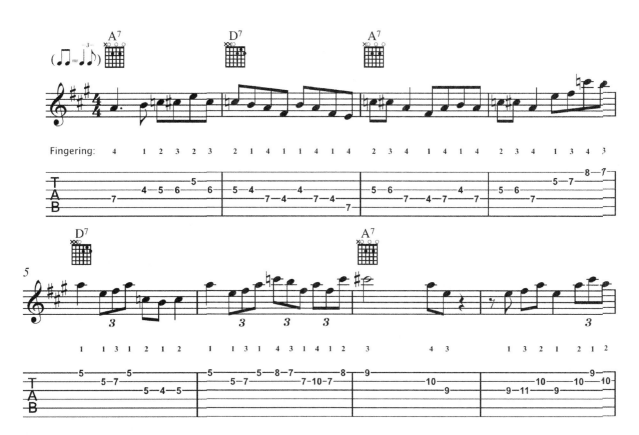

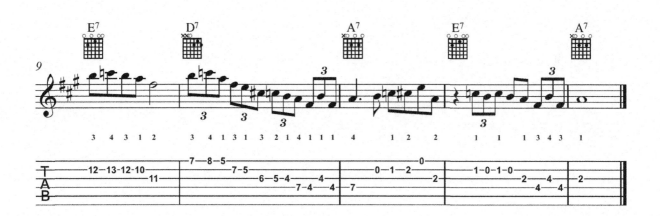

【A Major Blues Fingerstyle Demo】

Track 58

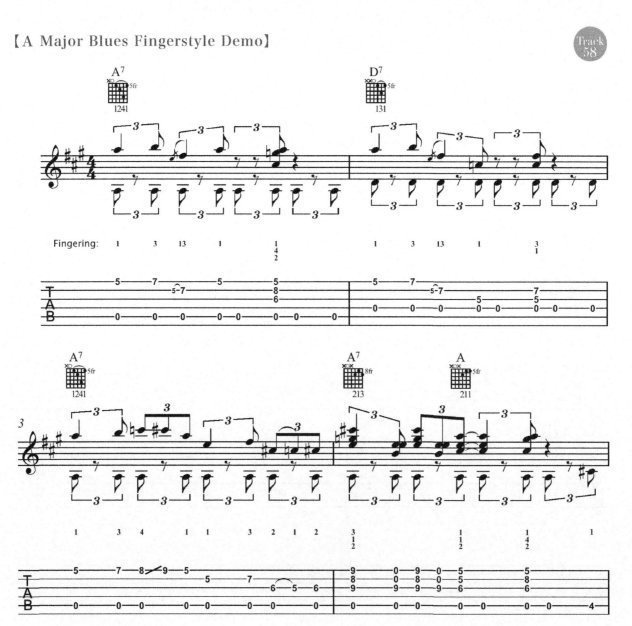

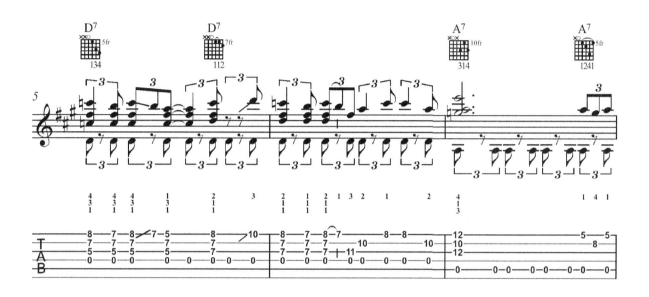

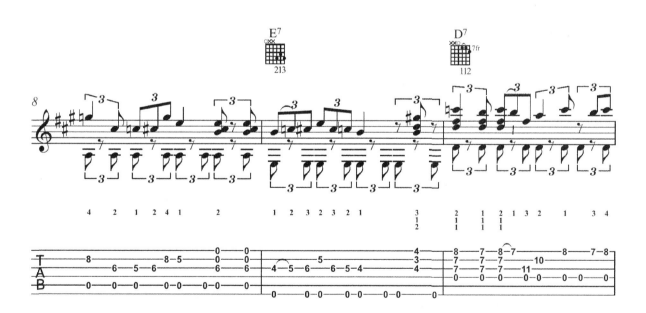

【E Major Blues Scale Demo】

Track 59

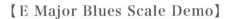

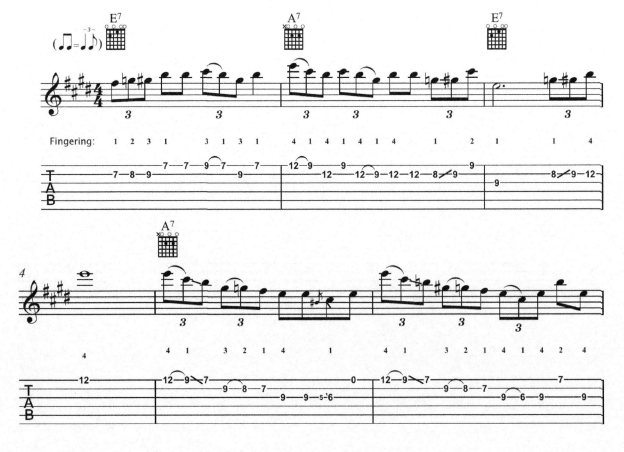

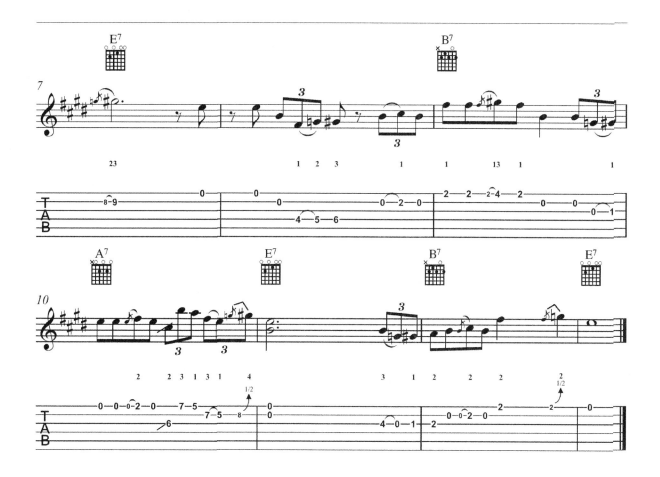

【E Major Blues Fingerstyle Demo】

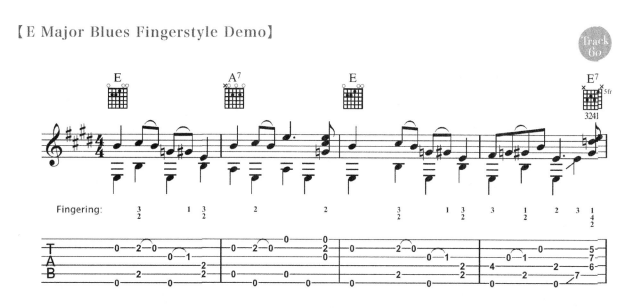

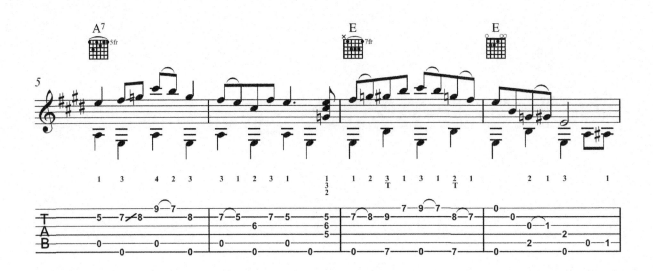

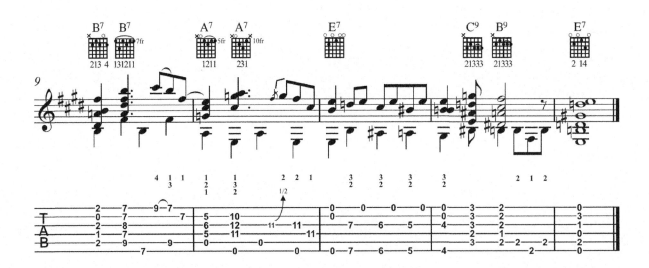

When practicing major Blues, you may also follow methods of the previous Blues position practice on your own.

◇ Flexible Changes of Blues Melodies

In addition to the above discussions we know that, in the basic Blues progressions, for scales we use other than the basic Blues scales, we can also choose to use major Blues scales to perform.

We learn from the previous demos that during the regular chord progressions of Blues, of the scales we can adopt, other than the basic Blues scales, we can also choose:

Blues scale   1   b3   4   #4   5   b7
Major Blues scale   1   2   #2(b3)   3   5   6

At this time, you probably may ask, is there other musical notes or scales to choose from？

And certainly, there is！ Here we would like to introduce practical applications of pentatonic scales in Blues.

【Major Pentatonic Scales of Individual Chord】

In basic Blues all Ⅰ7, Ⅳ7, Ⅴ7 contain formats of a major 3rd chord and therefore, we can analyze them individually and adopt their own individual pentatonic scales in a major key.

Format	1	2	3	5	6
Ⅰ7	1	2	3	5	6
Ⅳ7	4	5	6	1	2
Ⅴ7	5	6	7	2	3

Adding individual Blues notes:

Format	1	2	b3	3	5	6
Ⅰ7	1	2	b3	3	5	6
Ⅳ7	4	5	b6	6	1	2
Ⅴ7	5	6	b7	7	2	3

Now let's try to play a demo when matching each chord with its individual Blues scale in a major key:

< A Key Demo > :

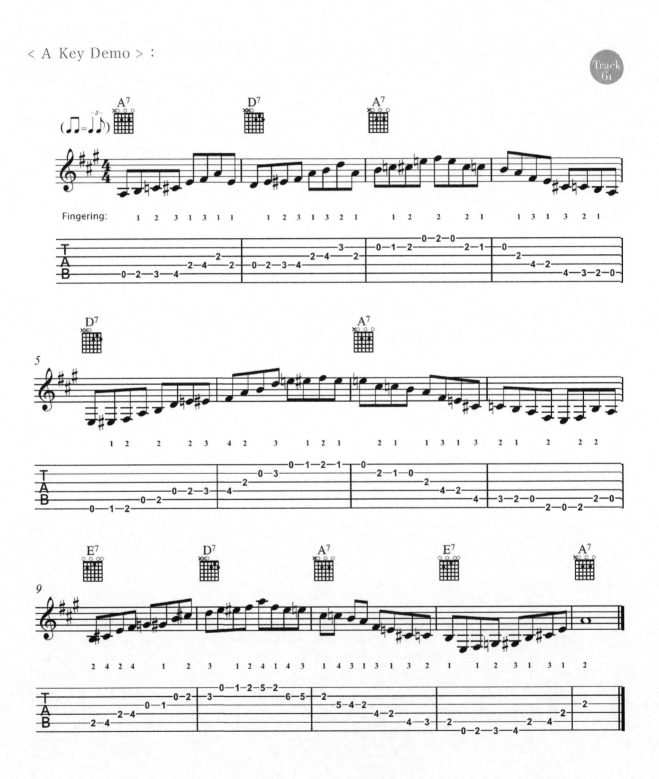

< E Key Demo > :

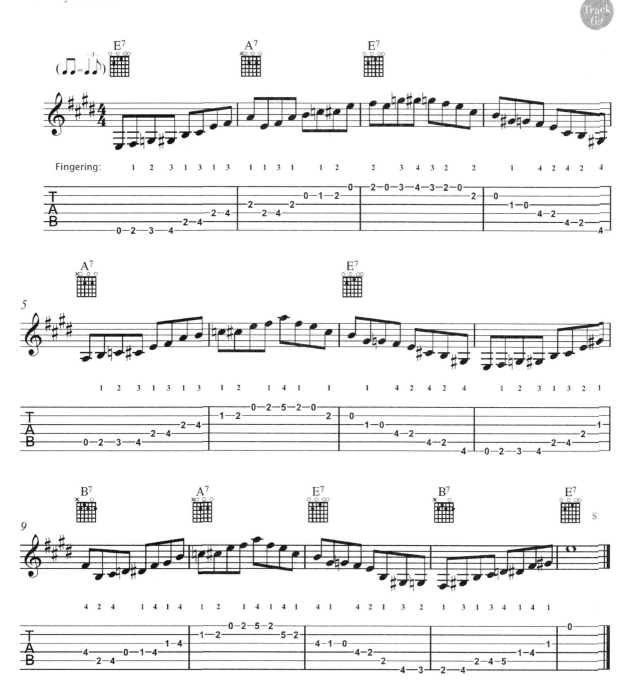

【Minor Pentatonic Scales of Individual Chord】

If this is the way it turns out, then can we also use the original minor pentatonic scale + Blues notes this way？ Let's try it now:

Format	1	b3	4	#4	5	b7
I 7	1	b3	4	#4	5	b7
IV 7	4	b6	b7	7	1	b3
V 7	5	b7	1	#1	2	4

< A Key Demo >：

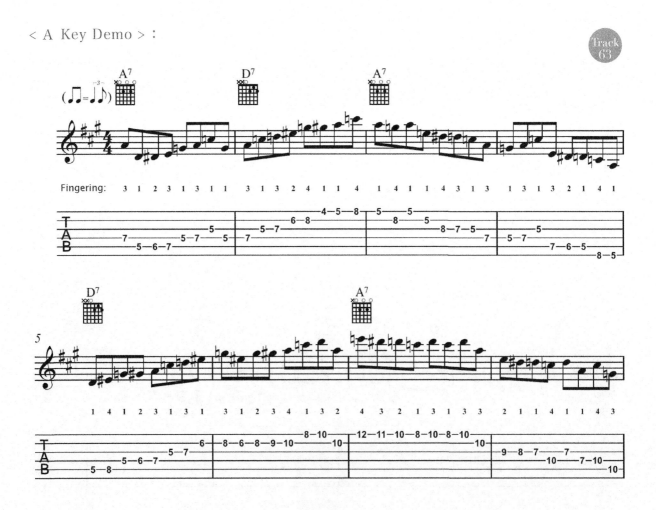

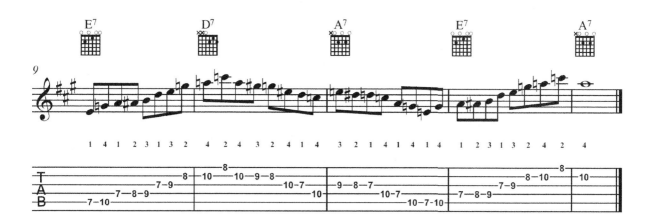

< E Key Demo > :

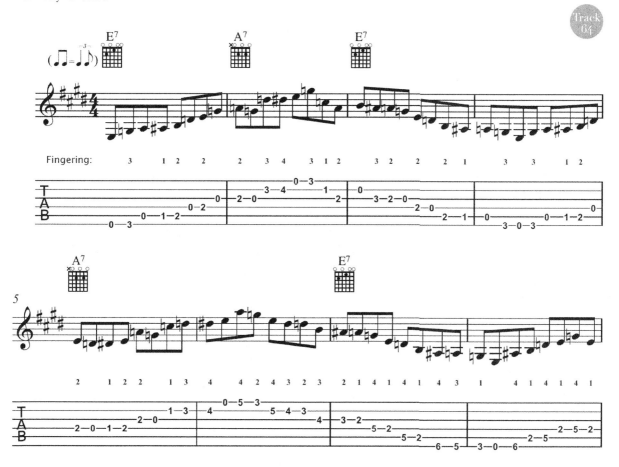

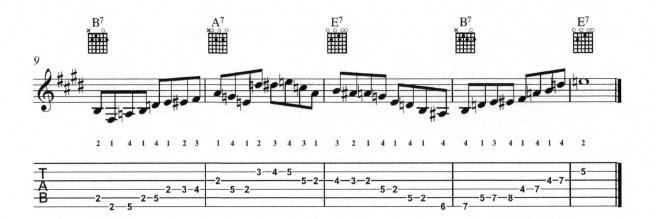

As a result, by adding previous scale methods, do we then have used all 12 musical notes？ Well...this is why music is so magical! By simply viewing this with musical notes, all the musical notes can be fully used; however, if you are aiming for playing good-sounding and atmospheric music, it doesn't work by directly playing all these musical notes. So what is important is that at where and how musical notes can be used and then result into what feelings or emotions？ It is not the formatted scale or what musical notes then should not appear at all...please be careful not to look for myth～

【Mixed Uses】

The demo below is for us to see what effects would be generated when we use all the above scales:

< A Key Demo >：

< E Key Demo > :

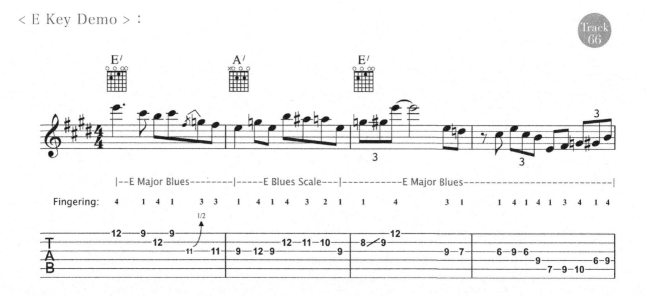

Track 66

...

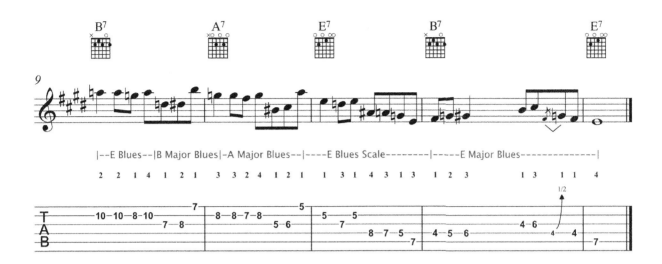

【Applications on Minor Blues】

The previous demos are all on regular Blues chord progressions, then what about minor Blues which mainly uses minor chords that also use the previous approach mixing with scales? Now, you can give it a try!

◇ Blues Melodic Improvisations

Blues music itself is the type that is often used for music improvisation. As its structure is simple, many variations can be done, and it is just like the uses of the above scales and musical notes. Therefore, this is also very suitable for musicians to exploit their abilities in improvisations.

Here below is a way for you to practice improvisation:

1. First choose Blues scale fingerstyle and musical notes of a certain fingering position, and start playing. And to play and sing along, especially when you feel special about the presence of one particular musical note. You then can stop on note and then hum, and play along for a few times.

2. You may start **rearranging** the playing order of these musical notes, and likewise hum along like what you used to do. If you discover a certain order for melody-playing that gives you a Blues feeling, then do feel free to try it for a few more times.

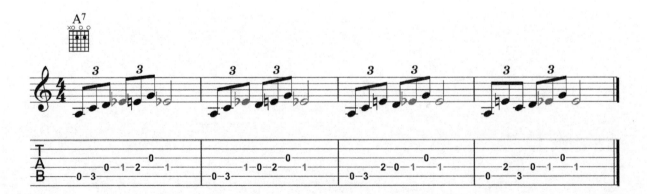

3. please take the previous long and short demos, and you can try to **do a little modifications** by sectioning (in one measure) the melodies. You can start from modifying just one musical note or likewise, rearranging the order of musical notes. You may simply hum along and feel the melodies which you have modified.

4. Playing out background accompaniment of Blues music and try to proceed to the above order of practice slowly.

If you would like to play good-sounding and authentic Blues music, you need to listen to more Blues music and to hum along just like learning to talk. And then, you can use your guitar to slowly play the melodies which you hum along with. Although the music may not sound authentic in the beginning, and this is just like when you are learning to speak a new language, you may have an accent, after a long while of exposure, you will slowly get the feel of Blues. Please make sure you are patient and ready to spend time on listening to Blues music non-stoppingly as well as continuous practices!

5. Blending with different scales

It's just like the very last two demos in the previous chapter in which we use different types of scale within different measures. It can be Blues scales, major Blues scales, or Blues scale which individual chord belongs to …, thus, here let's try practicing different scales in different measures.

< A Key > :

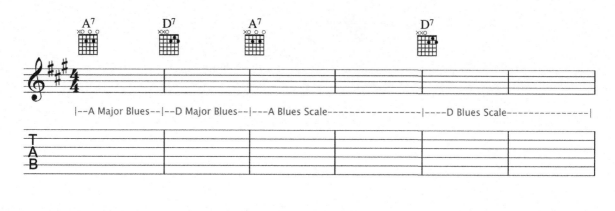

< E Key > :

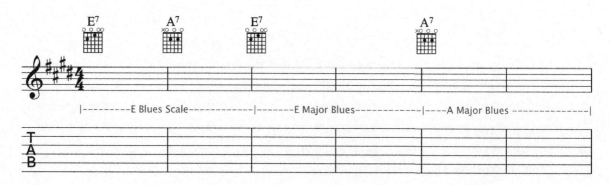

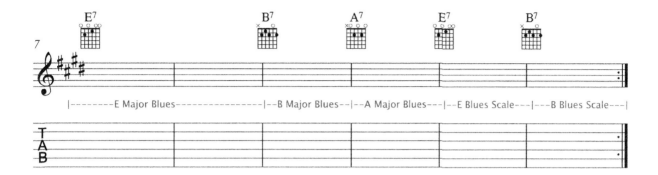

Next, you can try setting different use formats of scale on your own for practices.

When we feel there is no problem for individual scale changing, this doesn't mean it is the end of practice; instead, it is an official start for practice. Please with your fully-dedicated heart, you can start to feel whether the connection of musical sentences can be smooth and fluent to the progressions of background chords, and do the sentences sound good? Or whether the presenting timing of a certain single musical note has highlighted feelings of Blues music or its special effects.

Before we are able to use improvisation to play the next note, you then can predict the feelings and soundings of particular musical notes in your head and quickly decide on whether you would choose to play it or not. At this moment, you then start to get rid of chaotic playing and officially enter the beginning of Blues improvisation.

When improvising, do our brains really think seriously about which scales to play?

For playing a natural and fluent improvisation, under the timing of improvisation, your brain may only show musical notes and melodies instead of what scales we would like to use in the next measure.

The above practices are not designed for us to be prepared or switching to whichever scale when it comes to our minds instead, it is to develop our feelings and experiences for music. When we have an experience like "under such background music, we can play that particular melody or very good-sounding musical notes.", and what happens is that it's very likely for us to naturally play such musical phrases upon improvisation. And such musical phrases very likely may be certain scale-like melodies which we have practiced earlier.

After every sensation accumulates more, when improvising, you can then naturally feel how it's like to play the musical notes or melodies.

◈ Blues Fingerstyle Performance Applications & Improvisations

Previously, we again have learned many kinds of scale which are particularly for Blues music practices.
And next, let's add other voices into these scales and apply on fingerstyle performances!

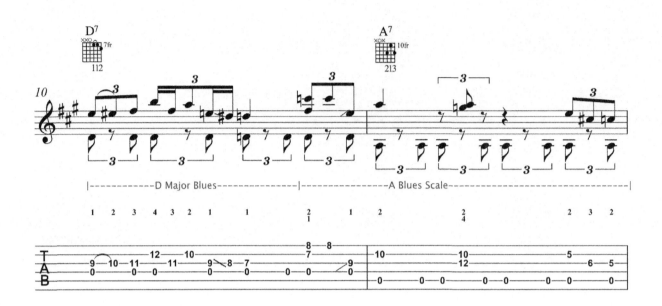

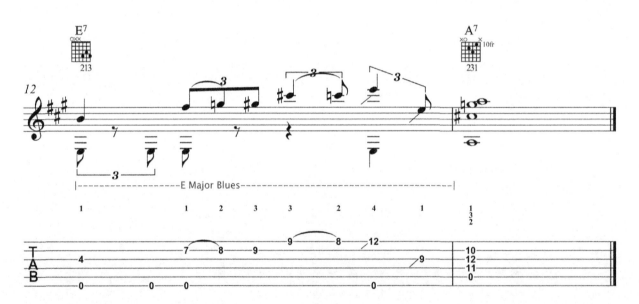

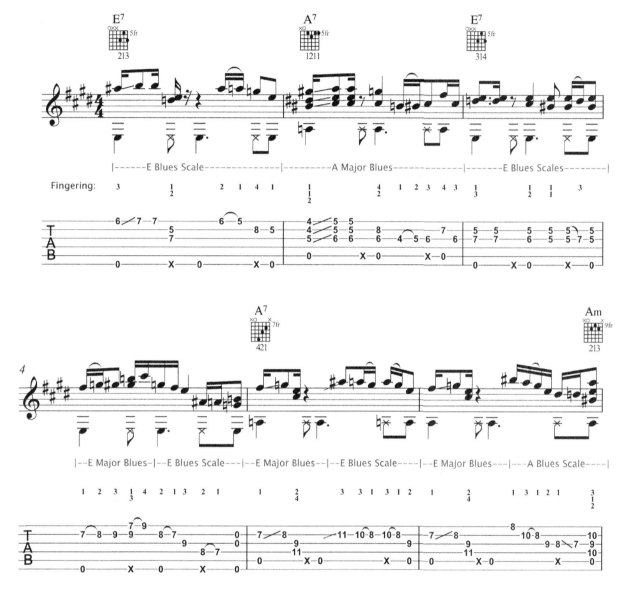

If you discover what I have demonstrated in the melodies has a note outside a marked scale, then that is to add a passing note or directly to obtain a music composing note of a certain chord. As we have explained in the previous section, it is not about certain scales that we use, and we are only be limited to use certain musical notes. All the 12 musical notes can be selected and used, and this is what I actually mean!

【Fingerstyle Blues Improvisation Performance】

If you are also in a good control of melodic improvisation, you can also try adding fingerstyle improvisation of other voices!

The differences between this and improvisation of previous melodies is that fingerstyle improvisation is limited to locations of other musical notes, however, as there's only three basic chords of Blues music, and also, we choose A key and E key which have an open note then it will not be too complicated and be hard to handle.

1. Two-voice improvisation playing

It is just like the beginning two-voice fingerstyle playing, simply we first treat root of chord as another voice. And however, in order to be more flexible when improvising melodies, we must know that besides root can be used by open note, the positions on strings of root that is of the same pitch.

< A Key > :

A7

While playing A 7 chords of I series and in addition to open A note of the 5th string, the other option would be the 5th fret of the 6th string that is of the same pitch to choose from. Therefore, by doing so, when we need to play the 5th string for a particular melody, we can also play an A note which is located at a different place for maintaining two-voice playing.

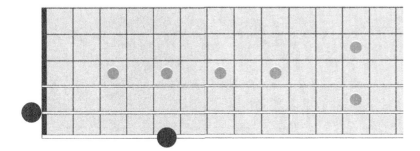

Etude Demo：

Track
69

While you are trying to practice improvisations on your own, please proceed to A7 root position change.

D7

While playing IV series D7 chord, in addition to open note D of the 4th string, there is still notes which have the same pitch on the 5th fret of the 5th string as well as the 10th fret of the 6th string to choose. This is because, if the 4th string is used as the lowest root note, then the remaining which are suitable for melodic improvisation would only have the 1st, 2nd and 3rd strings left. This way, if you are looking for improvising more musical notes in a short quick beat, and more limitations will be countered. Therefore, when we move to D7 measure, often position changes to bass notes is required.

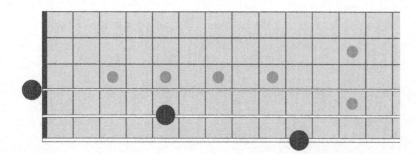

Etude Demo :

While you are trying to practice improvisations on your own, please proceed to D7 root position change.

E7 root is already on the 6th string; therefore, this would not quite be a barrier to melodic improvisations.

< E Key > :

B7

In E key, only B7 root of V series doesn't have an open note for you to use; therefore, we learn that it is much important to know the root position and make the right choices.

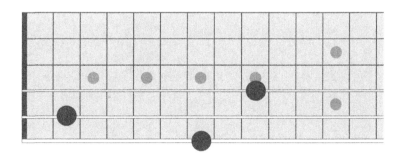

For a handling purpose in here, improvisation melodies would be extended to the 12th fret position by selecting B note which is one octave higher located at the 9th fret of the 4th string for bass voice presentation.

Etude Demo :

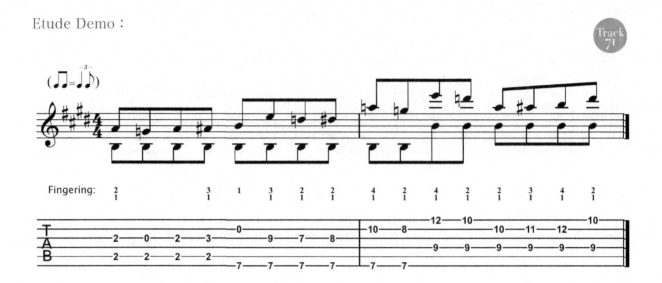

While you are trying to practice improvisations on your own, please proceed to B7 root position change.

2. Multiple voices improvisation performance

In this section, practice methods of improvisation are basically the same as the previous two-voice improvisation; however, it is only that we need to take into an additional consideration of one chord which requires a different string-pressing fret position. Moreover, as we have already known the positions of root note from the previous, certainly we then are able to know string-pressing method of chord fingerstyle for that particular position. For information like this, please refer to previous fingerstyle chart for inversion chords in previous sections.

As for practice methods, please once again review some fingerstyle demos in the previous sections which show the timing of chords or bass voices relatively to that of melodic lines. This timing is often in:

〉 **When playing improvisations, whether there are opportunities for free and available fingers to press chordal notes nearby.**

〉 **The intermission space of melodic phrases can be chosen to be made-up without affecting chord fingerstyles of the following improvisation musical phrases.**

Please slow down your speed and try one single measure practice of improvisation, and slowly you can find a whole set off fingering mode which belongs to your own multiple voices improvisation. And you can gradually feel the bliss of improvising freely!

◈ Unaccompanied Blues Improvisation Playing

The meaning of 'unaccompanied' simply means playing Blues melody only without playing other bass notes or alto voices. This kind of music often appears in old Blues music as there's no other accompanied music existing...this then gives people more of a lonely feeling.

Certainly the unaccompaniment Blues here does not mean we can play Blues musical phrases whatever we want and that is it. However, it means that **when we are playing simple Blues melodies, we also would want our audience to feel the moving motion of Blues musical form.**

Below we first provide a demo song and I invite everyone to listen to it. Let's see with a playing that way, would you feel that there is actually 12 Blues measure going on in the background?

A Key Demo /

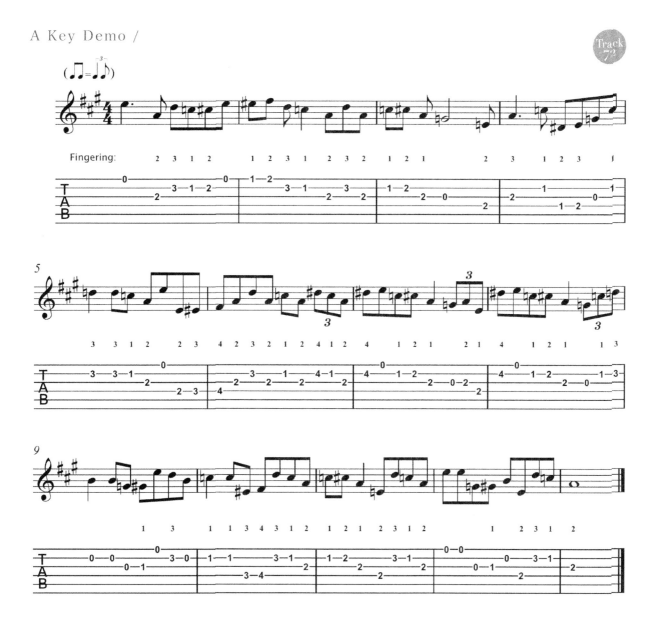

E Key Demo /

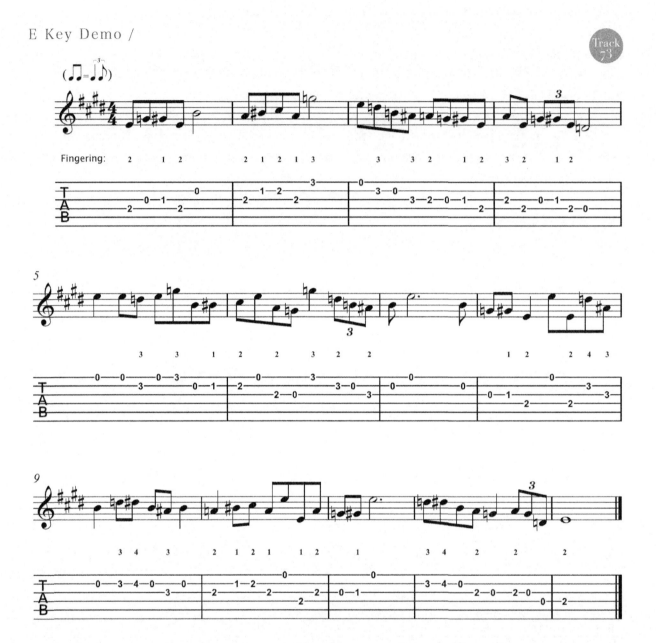

The above playings melodies actually use independent pentatonic scale wisely plus a structure of Blues note to achieve aurally a hidden moving feeling of the forms of music.

Let's see the format analyses of previous independent pentatonic scales, then we can discover that, when we follow chord progression to play the individual pentatonic scales, **as it contains different chord composing notes within the melodies**; therefore, this allows audiences to feel there is a particular type of chord that is ongoing.

An important concept here is that, **if the musical notes do not belong to the existing chord composing notes, you should try your best to play them less, or NOT to play them at all. Or you may play the notes with more techniques involved** (for instance, the notes can be treated as passing notes or be placed on a weak beat). This way, the audiences will not feel it's like a chaos in their aural experiences and thus they can't feel where current chord progressions are going to.

So you can try such single note method to practice improvisation, and see if you can use this approach to play longly Blues!

Additionally, there's also more advanced playing method, that is simply use minor pentatonic scale of one key to play moving feelings of a Blues scale. And that is you can use five musical notes to play a marching Blues. Let's all try this on your own!

A Key Demo /

E Key Demo /

Track 75

[Conclusions]

The door to Blues music is not as difficult and complicated as Jazz music; however, if you are aiming for a good playing, it is also a challenge for enriching its contents.

Starting from Chapter TWO, specifically to the contents of this book, readers need to spend more time thinking and practicing and find a comfortable methods on your own. Even several weeks are required for you to study a paragraph within a chapter, it is not too exaggerated at all. The reason is that it's impossible for every single method book to list out all practices. As a reader, you would need to understand the core methods and execute practices on key transposition or fret position. You then can slowly experience more Blues improvisation methods with more freedom.

Please pay attention to musical mantra and performances discussed in each chapter and that is the core for all self-evolutionary trainings. It is just like after what I have learned and self-practiced every method, when all the materials have been internalized, then what is remained is the instincts for musical notes and application techniques.

Therefore, please be patient and persistent in learning how to think.

Let's play on with our life!

Scott Su

Solo
Fingerstyle

Blues
Guitar

Your Personal Book of Solo Fingerstyle Blues Guitar

Author | Scott Su
Translator | Lynda Huang

Publisher | Scott's Time Capsule Music
Site | http://www.stc-music.com/
Email | web@stc-music.com

Printed in Great Britain
by Amazon